Quick Study

Editorial Offices: Glenview, Illinois • Parsippany, New Jersey • New York, New York
Sales Offices: Parsippany, New Jersey • Duluth, Georgia • Glenview, Illinois •
Coppell, Texas • Ontario, California • Mesa, Arizona

www.sfsocialstudies.com

Program Authors

Dr. Candy Dawson Boyd
Professor, School of Education
Director of Reading Programs
St. Mary's College
Moraga, California

Dr. Geneva Gay
Professor of Education
University of Washington
Seattle, Washington

Rita Geiger
Director of Social Studies and
    Foreign Languages
Norman Public Schools
Norman, Oklahoma

Dr. James B. Kracht
Associate Dean for
    Undergraduate Programs
    and Teacher Education
College of Education
Texas A&M University
College Station, Texas

Dr. Valerie Ooka Pang
Professor of Teacher Education
San Diego State University
San Diego, California

Dr. C. Frederick Risinger
Director, Professional
    Development and Social
    Studies Education
Indiana University
Bloomington, Indiana

Sara Miranda Sanchez
Elementary and Early
    Childhood Curriculum
    Coordinator
Albuquerque Public Schools
Albuquerque, New Mexico

Contributing Authors

Dr. Carol Berkin
Professor of History
Baruch College and the
    Graduate Center
The City University of New York
New York, New York

Lee A. Chase
Staff Development Specialist
Chesterfield County
    Public Schools
Chesterfield County, Virginia

Dr. Jim Cummins
Professor of Curriculum
Ontario Institute for Studies
    in Education
University of Toronto
Toronto, Canada

Dr. Allen D. Glenn
Professor and Dean Emeritus
Curriculum and Instruction
College of Education
University of Washington
Seattle, Washington

Dr. Carole L. Hahn
Professor, Educational Studies
Emory University
Atlanta, Georgia

Dr. M. Gail Hickey
Professor of Education
Indiana University-Purdue
    University
Fort Wayne, Indiana

Dr. Bonnie Meszaros
Associate Director
Center for Economic Education
    and Entrepreneurship
University of Delaware
Newark, Delaware

ISBN 0-328-09006-9

10-V016-12 11 10 09 08 07

Contents

Lesson 1: The American People

Vocabulary

culture way of life of a group of people

ideals important beliefs

ethnic group a group of people who share the same customs and language

census official count of all the people in the United States

immigrants people who leave one country to go live in another

Out of Many, One

The United States has a motto, or saying. It is *E Pluribus Unum.* This is Latin for "Out of many, one." This is a good motto for the United States because many different types of people form one country. Our country has a mix of many different **cultures.** All these different people are able to form one country because they share many **ideals,** or beliefs. These ideals include freedom of speech, freedom of religion, and freedom to live and work where we choose. Americans also believe in equal rights for all people.

Our Varied Population

Many **ethnic groups** are found in the United States. Ethnic groups are made up of people who share the same language and customs. Their families may have come to the United States from the same part of the world. People of different ethnic groups can be Americans. Every ten years the government counts all the people in the United States. This count is called a **census.**

Where We Came From

Immigrants have come to the United States from all over the world. They brought many different customs with them. Native Americans lived on this land before it became the United States. Europeans came to the area looking for land and freedom. People from Africa were brought as slaves. Many immigrants still come to the United States. Many are looking for work and freedom.

One Nation

The Pledge of Allegiance is important to the United States. It helps bring together the many different people who live in the country. The Pledge of Allegiance says that Americans believe in the ideals of freedom and fairness for all people.

Lesson 1: Review

1. 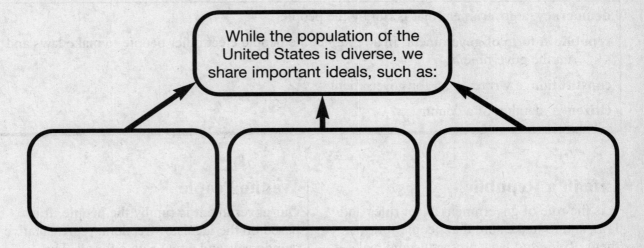 **Main Idea and Details** Fill in some examples of the ideals most Americans share.

While the population of the
United States is diverse, we
share important ideals, such as:

2. Why is *E Pluribus Unum* a good motto for the United States?

   _____

   _____

3. Why do immigrants continue to come to the United States?

   _____

   _____

4. What basic ideals unite most Americans?

   _____

   _____

5. **Critical Thinking:** *Point of View* How does the Pledge of Allegiance unite Americans?

   _____

   _____

   _____

Lesson 2: Government by the People

Vocabulary

democracy a government that is run by the people

republic a form of government; in a republic, the people elect other people to make laws and run the government

constitution a written plan for government

citizen a member of a country

Life in a Republic

It is the role of government to set rules and laws and to make sure that people follow them. Rules and laws protect us and make it possible to run a school, city, or country. The United States is a **democracy.** In a democracy, the people have the power to make decisions about government. The United States is set up as a representative democracy, or **republic.** In a republic, the people elect other people to make laws and run the government. This is different from a direct democracy. In a direct democracy, the people themselves make laws and run the government. Our republic is based on the United States **Constitution.** A constitution is a written plan of government.

The Role of Citizens

Citizens are members of a country. They play the most important part in the U.S. government. People born in the United States are U.S. citizens. People not born in the United States can become U.S. citizens. Citizens have several basic rights. Their rights include freedom of speech, freedom of religion, and the right to a fair trial. All citizens who are at least 18 years old have the right to vote. Citizens also have responsibilities. Some of these responsibilities are obeying the law, electing leaders, going to school, and respecting other citizens' rights.

We the People

Our government is run by the people. It is based on the ideals of freedom, representative democracy, and equal rights for all. The government has not always treated all people fairly. Yet we can change laws to protect all Americans.

Lesson 2: Review

1. 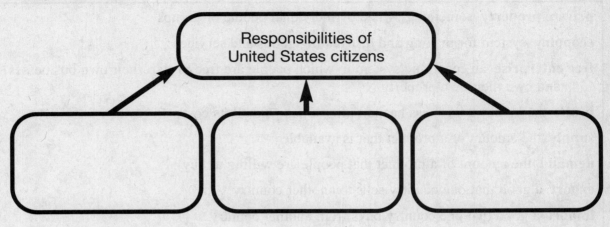 **Main Idea and Details** Fill in examples of important responsibilities that United States citizens share.

```
                    Responsibilities of
                    United States citizens
```

2. What is the difference between a direct democracy and a republic?

_____

_____

_____

3. What are some important rights and responsibilities of United States citizens?

_____

_____

_____

4. What are the ideals on which our government is based?

_____

_____

_____

5. **Critical Thinking:** *Decision Making* Do you think lowering the voting age from 21 to 18 was a good idea? Do you think it should be lower than 18? Use the decision-making steps on page H3 of your textbook.

_____

_____

_____

Lesson 3: Free Enterprise

Vocabulary

private property something owned by individual people or groups

economy system for making and distributing goods and services

free enterprise an economic system in which people are free to start their own businesses and own their own property

profit the money a business has left after it has paid all its costs

supply the amount of a product that is available

demand the amount of a product that people are willing to buy

export a good that one country sells to another country

import a good that one country buys from another country

consumer a person who buys or uses goods and services

entrepreneur a person who starts a new business, hoping to make a profit

How Free Enterprise Works

The U.S. **economy** is based on a system called **free enterprise.** Free enterprise lets Americans start their own businesses and also allows us to own **private property,** such as cars. Under this system, business owners may choose what they want to sell and how much to sell it for. Business owners generally want to make a **profit.** Prices for goods are based on **supply** and **demand.** Prices go up when demand is high and supply is low. This happens when many people want to buy something that is hard to get. Prices go down when demand is low and supply is high. This happens when few people want to buy something that is easy to get. People must consider opportunity costs, the value of the next best choice, when making a decision to produce or buy something. The United States trades many goods with other countries. The United States **imports** goods such as motor vehicles, electrical machinery, clothing, and computers and office machinery. The United States **exports** goods such as electrical machinery, motor vehicles, farm products, and computers and office machinery. Having

different resources available allows for specialization and means that countries need to trade with each other.

Benefits of Free Enterprise

Consumers can choose between many different products and decide how to spend their money. Free enterprise also gives consumers certain rights, such as expecting producers to supply safe, quality goods, and to be honest in their ads. Inventors also benefit from free enterprise. If they make inventions that people want to buy, then the inventors will make money. Thomas Edison was an inventor. Someone paid him a large amount of money for one of his inventions. With this money, Edison set up a laboratory where he worked on more inventions. Free enterprise also helps people called **entrepreneurs,** who want to start businesses and make a profit. In 1906 Madam C. J. Walker started a beauty products business and became a millionaire.

Scarcity

Scarcity means that there are not enough resources for all our needs, so careful decisions on usage must be made.

© Scott Foresman 5

Lesson 3: Review

1. 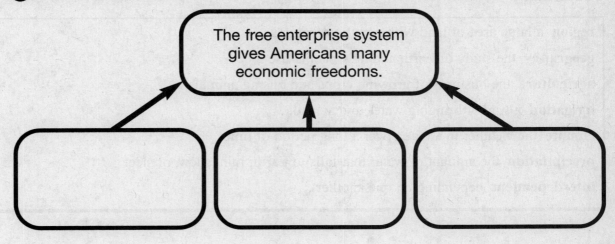 **Main Idea and Details** Fill in details of economic freedoms that Americans have.

2. How do supply and demand affect prices in a free enterprise system?

   _____
   _____
   _____

3. How did Thomas Edison benefit from the free enterprise system?

   _____
   _____
   _____

4. Name three goods that the United States both imports and exports.

   _____
   _____
   _____

5. **Critical Thinking:** *Decision Making* What decisions do you think Madam C. J. Walker had to make to start her business? Use the decision-making steps on page H3 of your book.

   _____
   _____
   _____

Lesson 4: Land and Regions

Vocabulary

region a large area of land with common features

geography the study of Earth and how people use it

agriculture the business of growing crops and raising animals

irrigation a way of bringing water to dry land

climate the weather in an area over a long period of time

precipitation the amount of water that falls to Earth; rain, snow, or sleet

interdependent depending on one another

Regions of the United States

The United States has five **regions:** the Northeast, Southeast, Midwest, Southwest, and West. Dividing the U.S. into these regions makes it easier to study the country's **geography.**

Northeast states are: Maine (ME), Vermont (VT), New Hampshire (NH), Massachusetts (MA), Connecticut (CT), Rhode Island (RI), New York (NY), New Jersey (NJ), Pennsylvania (PA), Delaware (DE), and Maryland (MD).

Southeast states are: Virginia (VA), West Virginia (WV), Kentucky (KY), Tennessee (TN), North Carolina (NC), South Carolina (SC), Georgia (GA), Alabama (AL), Mississippi (MS), Florida (FL), Louisiana (LA), and Arkansas (AK).

Midwest states are: Missouri (MO), Ohio (OH), Kansas (KS), Illinois (IL), Michigan (MI), Wisconsin (WI), Indiana (IN), Nebraska (NE), South Dakota (SD), North Dakota (ND), Minnesota (MN), and Iowa (IA).

Southwest states are: Arizona (AZ), New Mexico (NM), Oklahoma (OK), and Texas (TX).

West states are: Washington (WA), Utah (UT), Oregon (OR), Montana (MT), Wyoming (WY), Colorado (CO), Idaho (ID), Nevada (NV), California (CA), Alaska (AK), and Hawaii (HI).

People and the Land

Landforms, such as mountains or plains, affect how people use the land. Flat land is usually the best land to use for **agriculture. Irrigation** allows people to grow crops in areas that were once too dry to farm. The country's largest cities were built near bodies of water. Before there were cars or airplanes, people used the water to move goods and to travel.

Check the Weather

Different areas of the country have different **climates.** Temperature is part of an area's climate. The amount of **precipitation** an area gets is also part of its climate. Climates in the United States become cooler as you move north. The eastern half of the country is mostly humid. It gets more precipitation than the western half. The West is mostly dry.

Regions Work Together

The country's regions are **interdependent,** meaning they need each other. Different materials are often found in different regions. Regions therefore must work together to make a product. Links between regions are getting stronger because of computers. Computers make staying in touch easier for people in different regions.

© Scott Foresman 5

Lesson 4: Review

1. 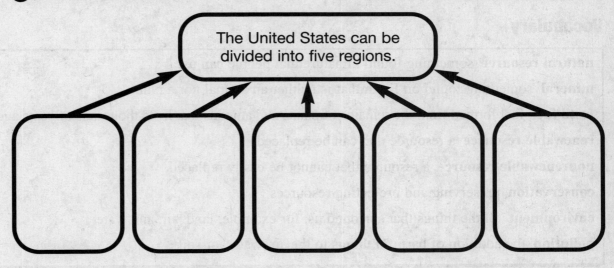 **Main Idea and Details** Fill in the states in each region of the United States.

2. What is one benefit of dividing the United States into regions?

   _____

   _____

3. Why are many cities located next to bodies of water?

   _____

   _____

   _____

4. Describe a major difference between the climates of the eastern and western parts of the United States.

   _____

   _____

   _____

5. **Critical Thinking:** *Draw Conclusions* Do you think the Internet has helped strengthen connections between the different regions of the United States? Explain your answer.

   _____

   _____

   _____

   _____

Lesson 5: Resources and the Environment

Vocabulary

natural resource something found in nature that people can use

mineral something found on Earth that is neither an animal nor a plant

fossil fuel fuel formed from the remains of plants and animals that lived thousands of years ago

renewable resource a resource that can be replaced

nonrenewable resource a resource that cannot be easily replaced

conservation preserving and protecting resources

environment all the things that surround us; for example, land, air, and water

pollution the addition of harmful things to the air, water, or soil

A Land Rich in Resources

The United States has many **natural resources.** Farmers use the land to grow crops. Wood from trees is used to build homes and make paper. **Fossil fuels** like coal, oil, and natural gas are used for energy. Fossil fuels are formed in the earth from remains of plants and animals that lived long ago. People also use **minerals** such as gold, salt, and aluminum. Minerals are neither animal nor plant.

Resources and People

Natural resources are very important to the United States. But the country does not have enough natural resources to last forever. **Renewable resources,** such as trees, can be replaced. **Nonrenewable resources,** such as oil, are harder to replace. We must protect and use each type of resource carefully. Protecting resources and using them carefully is called **conservation.** Natural resources are part of our **environment.** The environment includes all the things that surround us. Protecting our natural resources will help protect our environment.

Our National Parks

National parks are areas of land protected by the U.S. government. There are more than 50 national parks. They are set up all over the country. Yellowstone National Park was created in 1872. The Grand Canyon and parts of the Everglades are also national parks. National parks help protect our environment. Many types of plants and animals live in the parks.

Protecting the Environment

Pollution is the addition of harmful things to the air, water, or soil. Pollution is a problem in our environment. People can lessen pollution by recycling, or reusing things. Protecting the environment is important. We need natural resources for food and electricity. We also need clean air and water in order to be healthy.

Lesson 5: Review

1. 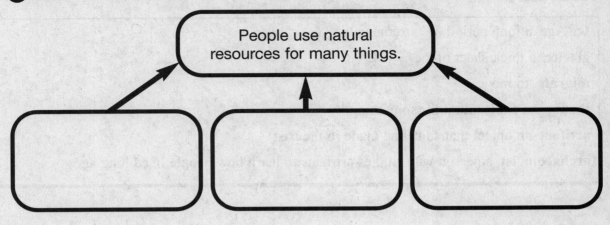 **Main Idea and Details** Fill in the three details that support the main idea.

People use natural
resources for many things.

2. What are three examples of mineral resources?

_____

_____

_____

3. How are renewable and nonrenewable resources the same? How are they different?

_____

_____

_____

4. How do national parks help to protect the environment?

_____

_____

_____

5. **Critical Thinking: *Point of View*** Do you think recycling is important in protecting the environment? Why or why not?

_____

_____

_____

© Scott Foresman 5

Lesson 1: Migration to the Americas

Vocabulary

Ice Age a long period of extreme cold

glacier a thick sheet of ice

migrate to move

theory an explanation for something

artifact an object that someone made in the past

archaeologist a person who studies artifacts to learn how people lived long ago

Moving into the Americas

About 20,000 years ago, Earth was very cold. This period is called the **Ice Age.** During the Ice Age, sheets of ice called **glaciers** formed. A large part of Earth was frozen under glaciers. The Bering Strait is a narrow body of water between Asia and North America. During the Ice Age, the Bering Strait became shallower. Land under the water was uncovered. This land formed a bridge between Asia and North America. Some people have a **theory,** or explanation, about how people first came to the Americas. Their theory is that hunters from Asia followed animals across the bridge to the Americas. Other people have a different theory. They think that people may have **migrated,** or moved, to the Americas by boat.

Ways of Life

The first people to come to the Americas lived in groups. Their main job was hunting. They killed animals such as mammoths and ate their meat. They used animal bones and skin to make tools, clothing, and shelter. Stone was also used to make tools. We have learned about these people through their **artifacts.** Artifacts are objects that were made a long time ago. People called **archaeologists** study the artifacts. They develop theories about how early people lived from these clues.

Changing Way of Life

About 10,000 years ago, the Ice Age ended. Earth's climate became warmer. Some of the bigger animals died out. The people then had to hunt smaller animals. They also gathered wild grains, root vegetables, berries, and nuts. About 7,000 years ago, these early Americans learned how to plant seeds and grow food. Farming let them settle in one place. They formed communities.

© Scott Foresman 5

Lesson 1: Review

1. **Summarize** Fill in the missing details from this lesson that support the summary.

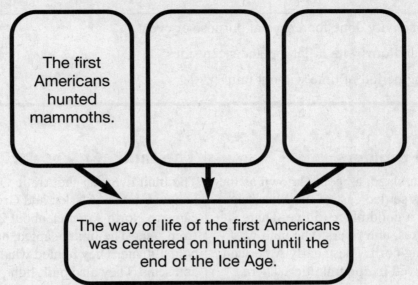

The first Americans hunted mammoths.

The way of life of the first Americans was centered on hunting until the end of the Ice Age.

2. Why do some scholars think people migrated from Asia to North America during the Ice Age?

_____

_____

3. How did the first Americans live during the Ice Age?

_____

_____

4. Why did hunters have to find new ways to get food when Earth's climate began to get warmer?

_____

_____

5. **Critical Thinking:** *Draw Conclusions* How do you think the early people discovered how to grow food?

_____

_____

_____

Lesson 2: Early American Cultures

Vocabulary

ceremony an activity done for a special purpose or event

mesa a high landform with a flat top and steep sides

drought a long period of time without rain

The Mound Builders

About 3,000 years ago, a people known as the Mound Builders settled east of the Mississippi River. This was a good place to live. There were forests, lakes, and rivers. The land was good for growing corn. These early American Indian groups lived in communities. There were three main groups of Mound Builders: the Adena, Hopewell, and Mississippians. They built thousands of mounds. They were used for burial places, to honor animal spirits, and to hold **ceremonies.** The mounds they left behind tell archaeologists that these groups were well organized. Many people were needed to build the mounds. Their artifacts show that trade was important to the Mound Builders. Objects from places far away have been found in the mounds. Seashells from the Gulf of Mexico and copper from the Great Lakes area are two examples.

The Anasazi

The Anasazi lived in what is now the Southwest United States. This area is dry. But the Anasazi were able to farm. They dug ditches to carry water from streams to the crops in their fields. The Anasazi built homes into the sides of cliffs. They also built apartment-style buildings on top of **mesas.** The Anasazi mysteriously disappeared. One theory is that they left because of a **drought.** The Anasazi may have moved to find water for farming. Some people believe that the Anasazi are the ancestors of today's Pueblo peoples.

The Inuit

The Inuit live near the Arctic Ocean in what is now Canada, Alaska, and Greenland. They came to North America about 2,500 years ago from Asia. The Inuit adapted, or adjusted, to the cold climate. They hunted whales, walruses, and seals. They also built light, one-person boats called kayaks. They used the kayaks for hunting and transportation. In the winter, some Inuit live in houses called igloos that are made of ice.

Lesson 2: Review

1. ⟳ **Summarize** Fill in the missing details that support the summary.

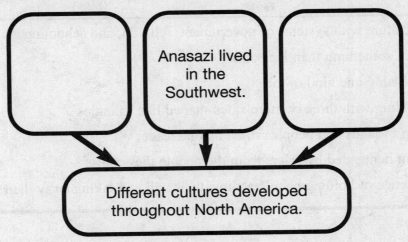

2. Why did the people known as Mound Builders build mounds?

   _____

   _____

3. Explain how the Anasazi were able to farm in the desert.

   _____

   _____

4. How did the Inuit adapt to life in the cold climate near the Arctic Ocean?

   _____

   _____

   _____

5. **Critical Thinking: *Compare and Contrast*** Compare and contrast the cultures of the Mound Builders, Anasazi, and Inuit.

   _____

   _____

   _____

   _____

Lesson 3: The Rise of Empires

Vocabulary

civilization a culture with systems of government, religion, and schooling

surplus more of something than is needed

specialize to do only one kind of job

pyramid a building with three or more sides shaped like triangles

empire a group of lands and peoples ruled by one leader

tribute payment demanded by rulers from the people they rule

slavery the practice of holding people against their will and taking away their freedom

The Maya

About 3,000 years ago, the Maya settled in what is now Mexico. They cut down trees to create fields. They grew corn and other crops. The Maya were successful farmers. They grew a **surplus** of crops. The extra food allowed some Maya to do other work besides farming. Some people could **specialize** in a job such as making baskets or jewelry. Specialization helped the Maya develop a **civilization** that had many achievements. The Maya studied mathematics and developed a calendar and writing system. They also studied the sun, moon, stars, and planets. The Maya built tall **pyramids.**

The Aztecs and the Inca

The Aztecs began to migrate south from northern Mexico in about 1200. They built the city of Tenochtitlan on an island in Lake Texcoco in the Valley of Mexico. Tenochtitlan grew to be a large city. The Aztecs built low bridges to connect Tenochtitlan to the land around the lake. They built floating gardens to have more farmland. They also made more farmland by carving steps into hills. Aztec soldiers fought and took over other people in the valley. Soon the Aztecs developed a large **empire.** They made the people in the empire pay them **tribute.** The Aztecs also took some people as tribute and made them slaves. The practice of holding people against their will is called **slavery.**

While the Aztecs were ruling in central Mexico, the Inca Empire grew in South America. The Inca also took over other people who lived nearby. The Inca built thousands of miles of roads. These roads united the parts of the Incan Empire. Good roads made good communication possible. Messengers from the capital city, Cuzco, could travel throughout the empire quickly.

© Scott Foresman 5

Name _____   Date _____

Lesson 3: Review

1. 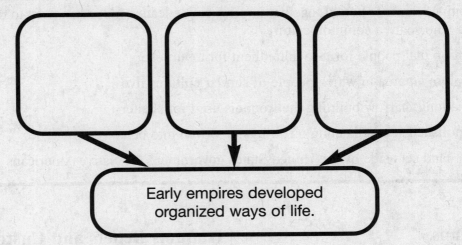 **Summarize** Fill in the details to the summary about the Mayan, Aztec, and Incan civilizations.

Early empires developed organized ways of life.

2. Name two achievements of the Mayan civilization.

   _____

   _____

3. What role did war play in the growth of the Aztec Empire?

   _____

   _____

4. How was the vast Incan Empire united?

   _____

   _____

5. **Critical Thinking:** *Compare and Contrast* How were the civilizations of the Maya, Aztecs, and the Inca similar? How were they different?

   _____

   _____

Lesson 1: The Eastern Woodlands

Vocabulary

tribe a group of families bound together under a single leadership; often used to describe people who share a common culture

league a group that people form to unite them for a purpose

cultural region an area in which people of similar cultures live

longhouse a long, narrow building the Iroquois used for shelter

wampum polished seashells hung on strings or woven into belts

reservation land set aside by the United States government for Native Americans

The Iroquois

In about 1580, five Native American **tribes** joined together to form the Iroquois League. A **league** is a group that unites for a special purpose. Each tribe sent 50 representatives to a Great Council. The Great Council made decisions for the entire League. The Iroquois Trail linked the League's lands. The trail ran through what is today New York State. There is a legend about how the Iroquois League began. Before the league formed, the five tribes often fought against one another. A man named Deganawidah wanted the five tribes to stop fighting and treat one another fairly. Another man, Hiawatha, got the tribes to bury their weapons and join together.

Living in the Woodlands

The Iroquois lived in the Eastern Woodlands **cultural region** of North America. Similar cultures develop within an area because of the resources there. The Eastern Woodlands had many resources. There were trees, animals, lakes, rivers, and streams. The Iroquois grew crops and hunted animals. They also fished in the area's waters. The Iroquois lived in longhouses made from trees. **Longhouses** were long, divided buildings shared by many families. The Iroquois also used trees to make canoes. They made clothing from animal skins.

Iroquois Beliefs and Customs

The Iroquois were thankful for the animals, plants, and world around them. The Iroquois made up stories and dances about the world around them. An Iroquois custom was to make **wampum,** or polished seashells hung on strings. Belts made of wampum were given as gifts, and wampum could be used to invite others to peace talks.

The Iroquois Today

There are about 50,000 Iroquois today. Many live on **reservations** in northern New York State. The Iroquois Great Council still meets. Some Iroquois men have become well known as builders of very tall buildings.

© Scott Foresman 5

Lesson 1: Review

1. 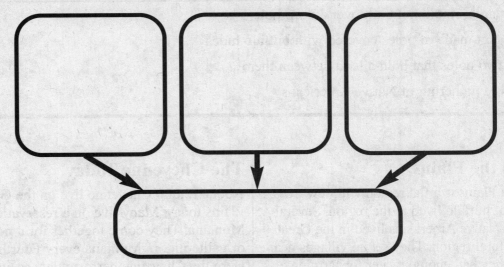 **Summarize** Choose the most important details from the lesson and organize them into a brief sentence. Fill in the chart below.

2. How did the Iroquois League make decisions?

_____

_____

3. How did the tribes of the Eastern Woodlands use natural resources to support themselves?

_____

_____

4. **Critical Thinking:** *Point of View* Explain the point of view of Deganawidah and Hiawatha about cooperation among the five tribes.

_____

_____

5. Where do the Iroquois live today?

_____

_____

Name _____ Date _____

Lesson 2: The Great Plains

Vocabulary

lodge a large, round hut built over a deep hole

tepee a tent made of poles covered with buffalo hides

travois two poles that hold a load between them

powwow a gathering of Native Americans

Life on the Plains

The Great Plains is a flat region with few trees. Millions of buffalo lived in the region. Several groups of Native Americans lived in the Great Plains cultural region. They set up villages near rivers so they had enough water for farming. They built **lodges** to live in. In summer and fall, the Plains people hunted buffalo. They used the buffalo for food, clothing, blankets, and other materials. While out hunting, the Plains people lived in **tepees.** They used poles to form a **travois** to carry buffalo meat and other goods. Dogs were used to pull the travois.

The Cheyenne

People from Spain brought horses to North America. In the 1700s the Cheyenne began to own horses. Using horses changed their lives. Horses made buffalo hunting much easier. Horses also helped the Cheyenne move more easily. They used horses instead of dogs to pull the travois. The Cheyenne began to move to different places for different seasons. They also rode horses in battles. Horses became very important to other Plains Indians too. Sometimes tribes captured horses from other tribes.

The Cheyenne Today

About 12,000 Cheyenne live on the Great Plains today. Many live on a reservation in Montana. They come together for a **powwow,** or gathering, in Montana every Fourth of July. Here the Cheyenne perform dances and play games that are hundreds of years old.

© Scott Foresman 5

Lesson 2: Review

1. Cause and Effect Fill in the missing causes.

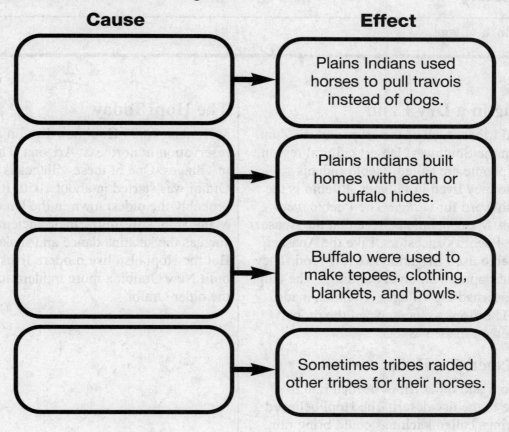

Cause		Effect

Plains Indians used horses to pull travois instead of dogs.

Plains Indians built homes with earth or buffalo hides.

Buffalo were used to make tepees, clothing, blankets, and bowls.

Sometimes tribes raided other tribes for their horses.

2. How did the travois help move goods?

_____

3. In what ways did the arrival of the horse change the way of life for the tribes of the Great Plains?

_____

_____

4. Critical Thinking: *Make Decisions* If you were a leader among the Cheyenne, how might you decide when it was time to move the settlement to a new area? Use the decision-making steps on page H3 of your textbook.

_____

_____

5. Where are Cheyenne reservations located today?

_____

Lesson 3: The Southwest Desert

Vocabulary

pueblo a village

Living in a Dry Land

Several tribes, such as the Hopi and the Zuni, lived in the Southwest Desert cultural region. These people are called Pueblo Indians because they lived in villages. **Pueblo** is the Spanish word for *village*. The Pueblo were farmers. Many people believe that the Anasazi are the Pueblo's ancestors. Like the Anasazi, the Pueblo used irrigation to grow food. They also built apartment-style buildings. The Hopi men governed the villages. The men made cloth. The Hopi women owned the property. The women made baskets.

The Need for Rain

The Hopi and other tribes needed rain to survive in the dry desert. The Hopi believed that beings called kachinas could bring rain. The people performed special dances to honor the kachinas and ask for their help. The dancers wore masks that looked like kachinas. The Hopi also performed the snake dance when they needed rain. Dancers would dance with snakes in their teeth. Then they let the snakes go. The snakes looked like streams of water. The dances were very important to everyone in the villages.

The Hopi Today

More than 7,000 Hopi now live on a reservation in northeast Arizona. They still live in villages. One of these villages is Oraibi. Oraibi was started in about 1050. It is probably the oldest town in the United States. Many Hopi still follow their ancient customs, such as the kachina dance and snake dance. But the Hopi also live modern lives. They built New Oraibi, a more modern town near the older Oraibi.

© Scott Foresman 5

Lesson 3: Review

1. **Main Idea and Details** Fill in the details that support the main idea from the lesson.

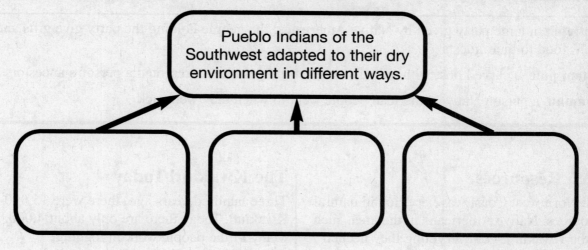

Pueblo Indians of the Southwest adapted to their dry environment in different ways.

2. How were Hopi villages governed?

_____

_____

_____

3. How were kachinas honored in Hopi ceremonies?

_____

_____

_____

4. What does the difference between Oraibi and New Oraibi tell you about the Hopi culture of today?

_____

_____

_____

5. **Critical Thinking:** *Draw Conclusions* Why do you think Pueblo people adopted Anasazi building styles? Explain.

_____

_____

_____

Lesson 4: The Northwest Coast

Vocabulary

potlatch a large party given by Native Americans; the people holding the party give gifts and food to their guests

totem pole a carved post with animals or other images that represented a person's ancestors

shaman a person Native American people went to when they were sick

Rich Resources

The Northwest Coast was very rich in natural resources. Native Americans in the area, such as the Kwakiutl, got everything they needed from the land and water. They built canoes from the area's many trees. They also fished and hunted for seals, sea otters, and whales. They could hunt and gather so much that they did not need to grow food. All these resources allowed the tribes to give many gifts to others. Giving to others and showing wealth was very important to the Kwakiutl. They held **potlatches,** or parties, where they gave away blankets and shields made of copper. They also carved tall **totem poles** and dugout canoes out of wood. The animals and other images on totem poles represented a person's ancestors. Totem poles also showed wealth. The Kwakiutl became master wood carvers.

Customs and Traditions

Shamans were important people in the Kwakiutl culture. The Kwakiutl people believed that shamans could cure them if they were ill. Both men and women could be shamans. Shamans helped people by performing dances. They wore carved masks. Special effects, such as smoke, were used to make the dances more exciting. Because food was easy to find, the Kwakiutl had time to carve and paint beautiful objects. Houses were made from cedar trees. Clothing was made from cedar tree bark and animal fur. The coastal climate was mild, so the Kwakiutl could often wear light clothing.

The Kwakiutl Today

Three hundred years ago, there were 15,000 Kwakiutl. Today there are only about 4,000. Many of the people work in logging, construction, or fishing. They continue to practice many of their older customs. They still hold potlatches. Shamans continue to serve the people. But the Kwakiutl also live in modern houses and go to see medical doctors.

© Scott Foresman 5

Lesson 4: Review

1. **Draw Conclusions** Fill in the boxes with the main facts from the lesson that support the conclusion about resources from the Northwest Coast.

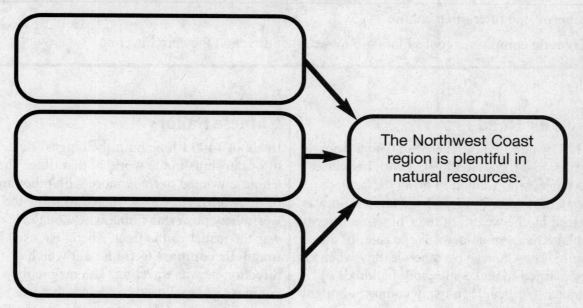

The Northwest Coast region is plentiful in natural resources.

2. Why did Northwest Coast people give potlatches?

_____

_____

3. What did shamans do to help people?

_____

_____

4. How much has the Kwakiutl population declined over the centuries?

_____

_____

5. **Critical Thinking:** *Predict* What changes might the Kwakiutl make in their culture if all the nearby trees were cut down?

_____

_____

_____

Lesson 1: Traveling Asia's Silk Road

Vocabulary

emperor the ruler of an empire

magnetic compass a tool sailors use to see what direction they are traveling

The Silk Road

In 1271 Marco Polo traveled to China from what is now Italy. He traveled with his father and uncle, who wanted to bring back goods from China to sell in Europe. Marco Polo was amazed by the wealth of the Chinese **emperor,** Kublai Khan. An emperor is the ruler of an empire. The Chinese became wealthy when they learned to make silk cloth hundreds of years earlier. People in many countries bought the silk cloth. The Silk Road was the main trade route between China and other lands. Silk, tea, and spices were the main goods that traveled on the Silk Road. People in Europe wanted the spices to give their food more flavor. Spices were also used to keep food fresh for a longer time. People also learned new ideas and customs on the Silk Road. Marco Polo's journey made people in Asia and Europe want to know more about each other.

Chinese Sailors

In about 1400 China built the biggest fleet of ocean ships in the world at that time. The Chinese wanted to trade more with other areas of the world. They also wanted to show the world how powerful China was. Zheng He was the leader of the fleet. Zheng He used a **magnetic compass** to figure out which direction he was traveling. The magnetic compass is a tool used by sailors that was invented in China. His ships sailed to the East Indies, India, the Persian Empire, Arabia, and the Red Sea to trade and explore. Everywhere the ships went, people wanted Chinese goods.

Lesson 1: Review

1. **Summarize** Fill in the missing details or events of the summarizing statement. The first detail has been provided as an example.

```
┌─────────────────┐   ┌─────────────────┐   ┌─────────────────┐
│ Marco Polo      │   │                 │   │                 │
│ journeyed       │   │                 │   │                 │
│ to China.       │   │                 │   │                 │
└────────┬────────┘   └────────┬────────┘   └────────┬────────┘
         │                     │                     │
         ▼                     ▼                     ▼
         ┌───────────────────────────────────────────┐
         │ Desire for trade led to more                │
         │ connections between continents.             │
         └───────────────────────────────────────────┘
```

2. What effect did Marco Polo's journey have on people of Asia and Europe?

_____

_____

_____

3. Name two goods that traveled along the Silk Road.

_____

_____

_____

4. **Critical Thinking:** *Cause and Effect* What were the goals of Zheng He's journeys?

_____

_____

_____

5. Look at the map on page 103. Which continents were connected by the Silk Road?

_____

_____

_____

Lesson 2: Africa's Trading Empires

Vocabulary

caravan a group of traders traveling together

pilgrimage a journey taken for religious reasons

astrolabe an instrument that helped sailors use the sun and stars to find their distance from the equator

Ghana, Kingdom of Gold

Trading kingdoms grew in West Africa more than one thousand years ago. In about 700, the kingdom of Ghana became powerful. There was much gold in Ghana. But Ghana did not have salt. Arab traders traveled across the Sahara desert in **caravans** to Ghana. A caravan is a group of traders traveling together. The caravans crossing the Sahara used camels. They traded their salt for Ghana's gold. The traders also brought their religion to West Africa. It was called Islam. Islam's followers are called Muslims. The kings of Ghana asked Muslims to help them rule the kingdom. Ghana's kings grew rich by taxing the traded goods. The kingdom of Ghana became less powerful by the 1100s.

Mali and Songhai

The kingdom of Mali was also in West Africa. Mali was larger than Ghana. It also had a lot of gold, but no salt. Mali was very rich from trade. King Mansa Musa ruled Mali in the 1300s. He went on a **pilgrimage,** or religious journey, to Mecca. Mecca is a city that is special to Muslims. Mansa Musa traveled with thousands of people. He brought 500 slaves to carry his gold. The king brought back Muslim teachers and artists to the city of Timbuktu. This made Timbuktu a center of learning. Between 1300 and 1500, Songhai became another powerful kingdom in West Africa. In the early 1500s, Songhai controlled more land than Ghana and Mali.

Connecting Different Parts of the World

People from different parts of the world were starting to learn about one another. People in Europe were learning about the people and geography of Asia and Africa. European mapmakers used the knowledge of travelers from around the world. The **astrolabe** was one Arab tool that helped sailors find their way by using the sun and stars. Maps and other tools made the connections stronger between different parts of the world.

© Scott Foresman 5

Lesson 2: Review

1. **Sequence** Fill in the missing events in this sequence chart showing the three major kingdoms in West Africa.

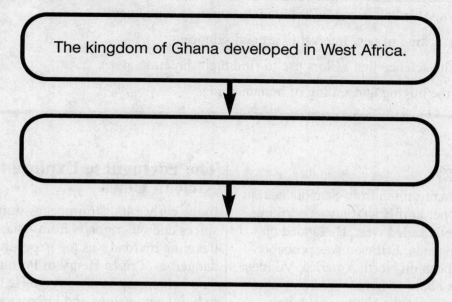

The kingdom of Ghana developed in West Africa.

2. Why did caravans cross the Sahara desert?

_____

_____

3. Why did Timbuktu develop into a center of Muslim learning?

_____

_____

4. What major resource did West African kingdoms control? Which important resource did they lack?

_____

_____

5. **Critical Thinking:** *Evaluate* Why did Mansa Musa travel with so many people and so much gold?

_____

_____

Lesson 3: European Explorers

Vocabulary

saga a long, spoken tale repeated from one generation to the next

Renaissance a time of new interest in art and science

navigation the science that sailors use to find their direction at sea

slave trade the buying and selling of human beings

The Vikings

The Vikings were sailors from Scandinavia, in northern Europe. Leif Ericsson was a Viking. In about 1000 he sailed west. He landed on what is now Canada. Ericsson was probably the first European on North America. Vikings lived there for about 15 years. We know about this journey because the Vikings told their story in **sagas.** Sagas are long stories that one generation tells to the next generation. Archaeologists have found huts, jewelry, lamps, and tools that the Vikings left behind.

The Renaissance

In about 1350 the **Renaissance** began in Italy. The Renaissance marked a new beginning in art and science. People were also interested in learning about the world around them. For example, Italians studied the ancient cultures of Greece and Rome. They also studied the cultures of faraway lands such as China. In about 1450 Johann Gutenberg developed a printing press in Germany. People could print large numbers of books quickly using this machine. Now more people could learn and read books. Europeans borrowed ideas, such as the magnetic compass, from other cultures. They used these ideas to build better ships. The ships allowed them to travel farther than ever before.

The Portuguese Explore the African Coast

In the early 1400s, Europeans wanted more spices and other goods from Asia. But traveling by road was too expensive and dangerous. Prince Henry of Portugal wanted to find better sea routes to Asia. He hired experts to build better ships and improve **navigation.** This is the science sailors use to find their way across the sea. These new ships then explored the western coast of Africa. The Portuguese brought home African gold and slaves. The **slave trade** grew. Other European countries began bringing African slaves to Europe.

A Sea Route to India

The Portuguese continued exploring. In 1488 Bartolomeu Dias sailed around the southern tip of Africa. He had reached the Indian Ocean! The king of Portugal named the tip of Africa the Cape of Good Hope. Ten years later Vasco da Gama sailed even farther and reached India. The Portuguese brought spices from India back to Europe. Portugal's sea routes made it a rich country.

Exploration Continues

Sea trade continued to grow. By the late 1400s, sea routes linked Europe to Asia and Africa. Europeans would soon travel to the Americas and meet the people who lived there.

Lesson 3: Review

1. **Draw Conclusions** List facts which lead to the conclusion shown.

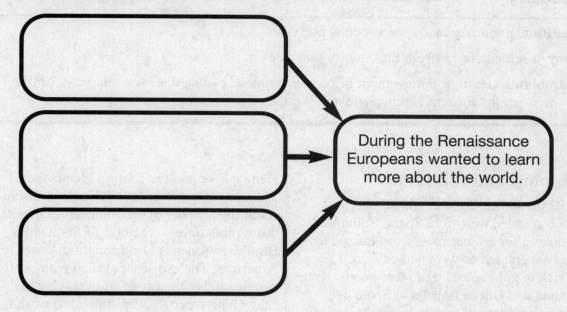

During the Renaissance Europeans wanted to learn more about the world.

2. What were some of the effects of the Renaissance?

_____

_____

3. What was the effect of Johann Gutenberg's new machine? What did it make possible?

_____

_____

4. **Critical Thinking:** *Cause and Effect* How did Prince Henry make Portugal the leading European country in the drive to explore other parts of the world?

_____

_____

5. What records of their attempt to settle North America did the Vikings leave behind?

_____

_____

Lesson 1: The Voyages of Columbus

Vocabulary

expedition a journey made for a special purpose

colony a settlement far from the country that rules it

Columbian Exchange a movement of people, animals, plants, diseases, and ways of life between the Eastern Hemisphere and Western Hemisphere

Columbus and the Taino

In 1492 the Italian explorer Christopher Columbus sailed west from Spain. Columbus was looking for a water route from Europe to the Indies. The Indies were part of Asia. They were rich in gold, spices, and other goods. King Ferdinand and Queen Isabella of Spain paid for the **expedition,** or trip, across the Atlantic Ocean. The king and queen believed that Columbus could find a cheaper and quicker way to the Indies. Columbus did not find the Indies. Instead he landed in a part of the Americas that became known as the West Indies. He claimed land in the area for Spain. He thought the land he claimed was part of the Indies. He called the people there Indians, even though they were actually named the Taino.

The Columbian Exchange

In 1493 Columbus led his second expedition to the Americas. He brought many ships with settlers, plants, and animals. He began a **colony** to make money for Spain. A colony is a settlement far from the country that rules it. People, animals, plants, diseases, and ways of life were exchanged between the Western Hemisphere and the Eastern Hemisphere. This movement was called the **Columbian Exchange.** Many of the things exchanged during this time were good for both sides. But the Europeans also brought diseases to the Americas. These diseases killed many native people, and their way of life was changed. Many native people were forced to work on sugarcane farms. Many were forced to give up their beliefs for Christianity.

The Impact of Columbus

Other European explorers came after Columbus. America is named for the Italian explorer Amerigo Vespucci. He sailed to the eastern coast of South America in 1501. In 1513 Vasco Núñez de Balboa, a Spanish explorer, reached the Pacific Ocean. In 1519 Ferdinand Magellan, a Portuguese explorer, led the first expedition to sail around the world. Many explorers and settlers had traveled to the Americas by the early 1600s. These settlers and the European countries they came from fought for control of land in the Americas.

Lesson 1: Review

1. ↻ **Sequence** Fill in the missing dates for each event on this chart.

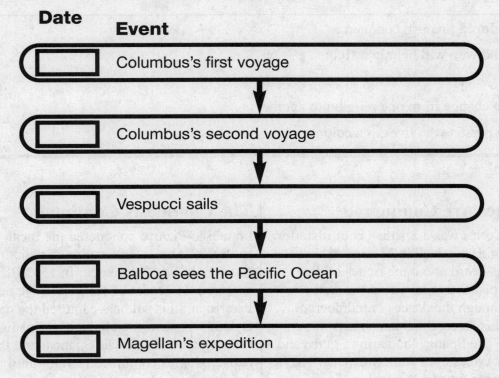

Date

Event

[ ]	Columbus's first voyage
[ ]	Columbus's second voyage
[ ]	Vespucci sails
[ ]	Balboa sees the Pacific Ocean
[ ]	Magellan's expedition

2. Why did Ferdinand and Isabella agree to support Columbus?

_____

_____

3. What was the goal of Columbus's second voyage?

_____

_____

4. How did the expeditions of Columbus lead to the Columbian Exchange?

_____

_____

5. **Critical Thinking:** *Draw Conclusions* How might life in Europe and the Americas have been different if Columbus had not journeyed here?

_____

_____

_____

Lesson 2: Different Worlds Collide

Vocabulary

conquistador a Spanish conqueror

ally a friend who will help in a fight

conquest the capture or taking of something by force

convert to change from one religion to another

colonist a person who lives in a colony

The Aztecs Are Conquered

Hernando Cortés was a Spanish **conquistador,** or conqueror. He arrived in Mexico in about 1519. Cortés heard about the riches of the Aztecs. He planned to take over the Aztec Empire. Although the Aztecs outnumbered Cortés and his force, the Spanish had some advantages. The Spanish had armor, guns, and horses. The Aztecs used stone weapons. They had no armor to protect themselves from Spanish bullets. Also the Aztecs were afraid of horses because they had never seen them before. Cortés also had **allies,** or friends, who helped him. Many native peoples did not want to live under Aztec rule. They joined Cortés to fight the Aztecs. Something else helped Cortés too. The Spanish brought the disease smallpox to Mexico. Smallpox killed many Aztecs. In 1521 Cortés defeated the Aztec Empire.

Founding New Spain

First, the Spanish conquered the Aztecs. Then, after their **conquest,** or the taking of something by force, the Spanish destroyed Tenochtitlan. Tenochtitlan was the capital city of the Aztecs. The Spanish founded the colony of New Spain in 1535. They set up a government, made laws, and built schools. Roman Catholic priests traveled to New Spain to **convert** the Indians to Christianity. People came from Spain to live in the colony. These **colonists** started farms, businesses, and gold and silver mines.

The Conquests Continue

Francisco Pizarro conquered the Incan Empire for Spain. The Incan Empire was south of Mexico, in South America. In 1532 Pizarro captured the leader of the Incas. The next year, Pizarro and his soldiers captured the capital. By 1535 Pizarro founded a new Spanish colony named Peru. The Spanish and the native peoples continued to fight until most of the native peoples were defeated. Then a new culture developed. It was a mixture of Spanish culture and the culture of the native peoples.

© Scott Foresman 5

Lesson 2: Review

1.  **Sequence** Place these events in the correct sequence and fill in the missing dates.

Date   **Event**

New Spain is established

Tenochtitlán falls

Cortés arrives in Mexico

Pizarro conquers the Incas

2. What were the key advantages of Hernando Cortés in defeating the Aztecs?

_____

_____

3. Why did Spain send priests to New Spain?

_____

_____

4. How long did it take Pizarro to conquer the Incan Empire?

_____

_____

5. **Critical Thinking:** *Problem Solving* The Spanish set up a government to rule New Spain. Think about how you would rule this colony. Write a short description of one problem and a suggested solution. Use the problem-solving steps on page H3 of your textbook.

_____

_____

© Scott Foresman 5

Lesson 3: Life in New Spain

Vocabulary

society a group of people forming a community

plantation a large farm with many workers who live on the land they work

encomienda a grant that gave a wealthy settler control of the native people who lived on an area of land

missionary a person who teaches his or her religion to others who have different beliefs

mission a religious settlement where missionaries live and work

The Search for Gold

The Spanish traveled north of Mexico in search of treasure. They had heard about rich kingdoms in the area. Cíbola was one of these kingdoms. The story of Cíbola was told by an enslaved African sailor. He had searched for the kingdom, but he died without finding it. The governor of New Spain then sent Francisco Vásquez de Coronado to find Cíbola. The kingdom was never found because it did not exist. Other Spanish explorers traveled to the Americas. Juan Ponce de León landed on the Florida peninsula in 1513. In 1540 Hernando de Soto became the first European to reach the Mississippi River.

Society in New Spain

By the late 1500s, **society** in New Spain had four different groups. The most powerful group was the people who were born in Spain. They were called peninsulares. The second group was people who had a Spanish background, but were born in the Americas. The third group was made up of people with a mixed background. The lowest group in the society was the native people and Africans who did not have Spanish ancestors. Peninsulares owned **plantations,** or large farms with many workers. Some peninsulares were given **encomiendas.** Encomiendas

were grants that gave landowners control over native people living on the land. The peninsulares made a lot of money because of slave labor.

More Changes for Native Peoples

Native people on encomiendas worked as farm workers, miners, and servants. Many of them were treated poorly. Some **missions,** or religious settlements, were given encomiendas. **Missionaries** taught Christianity to native people. Priests built missions throughout New Spain. Some missionaries mistreated native people. Bartolomé de Las Casas was a priest. In 1527 he defended the rights of native people living on missions.

Slavery in the Americas

Many native people died from disease and overwork. Then, the Spanish replaced them with enslaved Africans. In 1512 the first African slaves were brought to Hispaniola, a Caribbean island. At first, Las Casas supported African slavery. He later changed his opinion. African slave labor became an important part of the economy in New Spain.

© Scott Foresman 5

Lesson 3: Review

1. 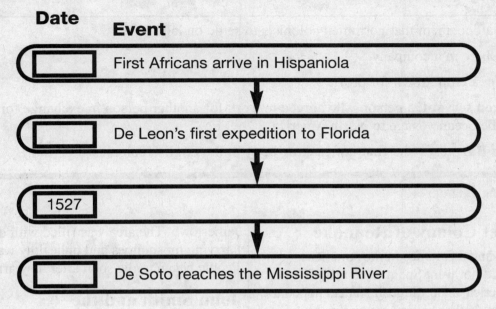 **Sequence** Fill in either the missing dates or the missing events from this time line.

Date   **Event**

| | First Africans arrive in Hispaniola |

| | De Leon's first expedition to Florida |

| 1527 | |

| | De Soto reaches the Mississippi River |

2. How did stories about Cíbola affect Spanish explorers?

_____

_____

3. How did the structure of society in New Spain benefit the Spanish?

_____

_____

4. How did conquest by the Spanish change life for the native peoples?

_____

_____

5. **Critical Thinking:** *Point of View* Summarize the point of view of Las Casas about native people on the encomiendas.

_____

_____

Lesson 1: Hard Times in Virginia

Vocabulary

charter a document that permitted colonists to settle on land

stock a share in a company

cash crop a crop grown for profit

indentured servant a person who agreed to work for another person in exchange for the cost of the ocean voyage to North America

House of Burgesses the first law-making body in the English colonies

The Lost Colony of Roanoke

England wanted colonies in the Americas. England did not want Spain to control all of North America. Also, English leaders hoped to find gold and other natural resources. An English colony set up on Roanoke Island in 1585 was not a success. In 1587 John White started another colony on Roanoke Island. White returned to England. When he went back to the island in 1590, the colonists were gone. Roanoke is called "The Lost Colony" because no one knows what happened to the colonists.

The Battle of the Spanish Armada

Spain did not like England moving into North America. English sea captains had also been taking riches from Spanish ships. Spain attacked England in 1588. The Spanish Armada, a huge fleet of warships, sailed to England. The English navy defeated the Spanish Armada using smaller, faster ships with powerful guns.

The Jamestown Colony

In 1606 the Virginia Company was formed to set up a colony in North America. **Stocks,** or shares in the company, were sold to pay for setting up the colony. The company received a **charter,** or land grant, from King James I of England. In 1607 colonists settled in an area on the eastern coast of Virginia and named the area

Jamestown. The area was filled with disease-carrying mosquitoes and unhealthy water. People began to die soon after they arrived.

John Smith and the "Starving Time"

Some colonists in Jamestown spent their time looking for gold instead of setting up their colony. John Smith became leader of Jamestown. He made the colonists build houses, dig wells, plant crops, and fish. Smith left Jamestown in 1609. After he left, many people in Jamestown died. In 1610 new settlers and supplies from England helped save the settlers.

Tobacco Helps Jamestown Grow

Tobacco became Virginia's first **cash crop,** a crop grown for profit. Farms grew quickly. The farms needed more workers. This brought **indentured servants,** or people who worked to pay off the cost of the trip from England.

Self-Government in Virginia

The Virginia Company set up the **House of Burgesses.** It was the first law-making body in an English colony. The House of Burgesses began the tradition of self-government in the English colonies.

© Scott Foresman 5

Lesson 1: Review

1. **Compare and Contrast** Fill in the diagram below comparing and contrasting these details about Roanoke and Jamestown:
   - Why did some English leaders want to build colonies in North America?
   - How did John Smith help the Jamestown colony?
   - How did tobacco help Jamestown grow?

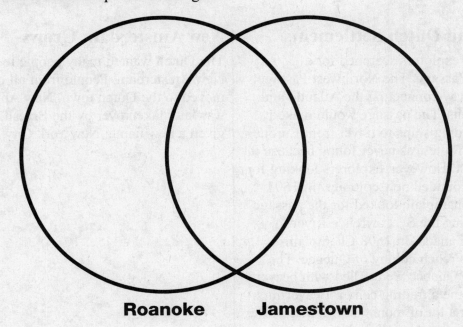

Roanoke   **Jamestown**

2. Why did England want to begin a colony on North America's eastern shore?

   _____

   _____

3. How did England defeat the Spanish Armada in 1588?

   _____

   _____

4. Why did Jamestown almost fail? How was it able to survive?

   _____

   _____

5. **Critical Thinking:** *Make Decisions* Do you think the House of Burgesses was the best type of government for the Jamestown colony? Why or why not?

   _____

   _____

Lesson 2: New European Colonies

Vocabulary

Northwest Passage a waterway connecting the Atlantic and Pacific Oceans

French and Dutch Settlements

In the 1600s explorers searched for a **Northwest Passage.** The Northwest Passage was a waterway connecting the Atlantic and Pacific Oceans. The passage would make it easier for trading ships to travel from Europe to Asia. The route was never found because it does not exist. However, explorers looking for the passage founded new colonies. In 1603 Samuel de Champlain looked for the passage while exploring the St. Lawrence River in present-day Canada. In 1608 Champlain founded the French colony of Quebec. The lands around Quebec were filled with beavers. Quebec became a trading center. Beaver furs were sold for a lot of money in Europe. More French colonies grew up in other areas. These colonies became known as New France. Dutch leaders sent Henry Hudson to search for new water routes to Asia. This Englishman searched along the North American coast. He explored 150 miles of what later became known as the Hudson River. He claimed the land for the Dutch. The Dutch colonies in North America were called New Netherland. New Amsterdam was a Dutch town built on Manhattan Island in 1624. The Dutch controlled trade on the Hudson River from New Amsterdam.

New Amsterdam Grows

The Dutch wanted many people to move to New Amsterdam. People from all over Europe moved to the Dutch town. New Amsterdam was later taken over by the British. It was given a new name: New York City.

Lesson 2: Review

1. **Cause and Effect** Fill in the chart below by listing one important effect of each cause.

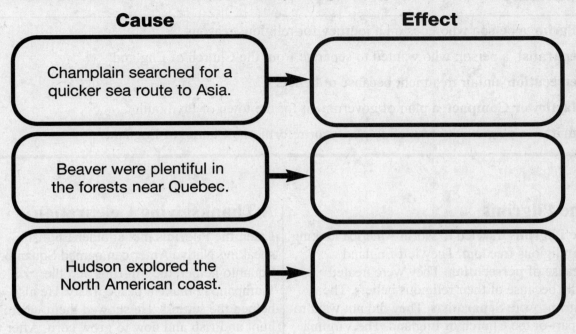

Cause	Effect
Champlain searched for a quicker sea route to Asia.	
Beaver were plentiful in the forests near Quebec.	
Hudson explored the North American coast.	

2. How did the search for a Northwest Passage lead to the founding of New France and New Netherland?

_____

_____

3. What kind of benefits did France gain from its colony of New France?

_____

_____

4. Why was New Amsterdam a good location for a city?

_____

_____

5. **Critical Thinking:** *Drawing Conclusions* Do you think Native Americans played an important role in the growth of French and Dutch settlements? Explain.

_____

_____

Lesson 3: The First Colonies

Vocabulary

Pilgrim a person who goes on a journey for religious reasons

Separatist a person who wanted to separate from the Church of England

persecution unfair treatment because of beliefs

Mayflower Compact a plan of government for the town of Plymouth

Puritan a person who wanted to purify, or reform, the Church of England

The Pilgrims

The **Pilgrims** traveled to North America looking for religious freedom. They left England because of **persecution.** They were treated badly because of their religious beliefs. The Pilgrims were **Separatists.** They did not want to be part of the Church of England. The Virginia Company gave the Pilgrims permission to start their settlement in Virginia. William Bradford led the Pilgrims.

The *Mayflower*

In 1620 about 100 Pilgrims left England. They sailed their ship, the *Mayflower,* across the Atlantic Ocean. They landed in New England. They decided to stay there instead of Virginia. The Pilgrims made a plan of government for their future settlement. The plan was called the **Mayflower Compact.** It said that the Pilgrims would make fair and equal laws for their colony. The Pilgrims settled in Plymouth in today's Massachusetts. The Pilgrims met a Native American named Samoset who spoke English. They began a friendship with the Wampanoag people.

A Thanksgiving Celebration

Later, the Pilgrims met another English-speaking Native American named Squanto. Squanto helped the Pilgrims and the Wampanoag make a peace treaty. He also helped the settlers. He showed them where to hunt and fish and how to grow corn. After their first harvest, the Pilgrims held a celebration of thanksgiving with the Wampanoag.

The Puritans Arrive

The **Puritans** also left England looking for religious freedom. They were persecuted because they wanted to change the Church of England. John Winthrop led the Puritans. He wanted to build a colony in New England. In this colony, the Puritans could worship as they wanted. They would teach others to live good lives by setting an example. In about 1628 the Puritans set up the Massachusetts Bay Colony. Its main town was Boston.

The Puritan Way of Life

Puritan settlements were carefully planned. A meetinghouse was built in the center of town. Religious services and town meetings were held in the meetinghouse. Each family was given land for a house and farm. In 1635 the Puritans built the first public school in the English colonies. They wanted children to be able to read the Bible and understand community laws.

© Scott Foresman 5

Lesson 3: Review

1. **Compare and Contrast** Fill in the chart comparing and contrasting these details:

   • Name of group and year founded
   • Group's leader
   • Reason people came to colony

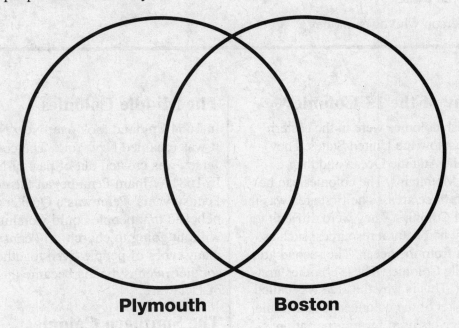

Plymouth   **Boston**

2. What was the main reason that the Pilgrims came to New England?

   _____

   _____

3. What was the purpose of the Mayflower Compact?

   _____

   _____

4. How did the Native Americans help the Pilgrims?

   _____

   _____

5. **Critical Thinking: *Point of View*** John Winthrop wrote that the Puritan colony would be like "a City upon a hill, the eyes of all people are on us." Explain how this statement reflects the Puritan view about the colony.

   _____

   _____

Lesson 4: The 13 English Colonies

Vocabulary

dissenter a person whose views are different from those held by most people

proprietor an owner

debtor a person who owes money

Geography of the 13 Colonies

The 13 English colonies were in the eastern part of what is now the United States. They lay between the Atlantic Ocean and the Appalachian Mountains. The colonies can be separated into three areas. The first area was the New England Colonies. They were difficult to farm, but they had natural resources, such as trees and fish from the ocean. The second area was the Middle Colonies. These colonies grew a lot of wheat. This is why the area was called "the breadbasket of the colonies." The Middle Colonies had rivers used for transportation. Farming was also very important in the third area, the Southern Colonies. These colonies grew crops such as tobacco. The area had many rivers.

New England Colonies

Many Puritan settlements were built in Massachusetts during the 1630s. Puritan settlers had to follow the laws of the settlement. Yet not everyone agreed with the laws. Roger Williams was a minister in Massachusetts. He believed that the government should not punish people for their beliefs. Williams was a **dissenter,** or a person with unpopular views. In 1636 Williams founded the settlement of Providence in the colony that became Rhode Island. In Providence settlers could practice any religion. Anne Hutchinson was another dissenter. Puritan leaders forced her to leave Massachusetts. Thomas Hooker was a Puritan minister. He founded the colony of Connecticut. He and his followers wanted religious freedom. They also wanted fertile land for farming.

The Middle Colonies

In 1664 England took over New Netherland. It was renamed New York. The colony of New Jersey was created out of part of New York. In 1681 William Penn began the colony of Pennsylvania. Penn was a Quaker. Quakers believed that people could worship God without going to church. In Pennsylvania many types of people lived together. Part of southern Pennsylvania became the colony of Delaware.

The Southern Colonies

The colony of Maryland was a safe place for both Catholics and Protestants. Maryland was a proprietary colony. This means that the land was controlled by an individual or a group of **proprietors,** or owners. In 1663 proprietors set up the colony of Carolina. James Oglethorpe founded the last of the English colonies, Georgia. It was set up to help **debtors,** or people who owed money. Georgia was north of Spanish Florida. Georgia could help protect the other English colonies if the Spanish attacked them.

Growing Colonies

The English colonies grew quickly. The largest cities were Boston, Philadelphia, and New York.

Lesson 4: Review

1. **Compare and Contrast** Fill in the chart below for two of the three regions—New England, Middle, and Southern Colonies. Compare and contrast based on such topics as geography and reason for founding.

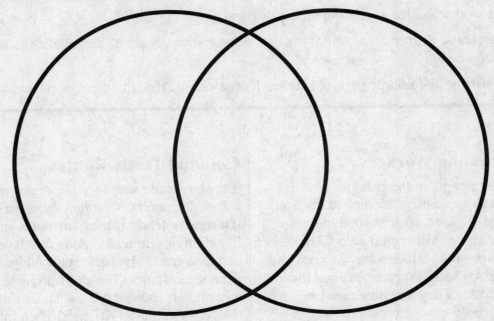

2. Why were the Middle Colonies known as "the breadbasket of the colonies"?

_____

_____

3. Explain how one New England colony was founded by a dissenter.

_____

_____

4. What attracted settlers to Georgia?

_____

_____

5. **Critical Thinking:** *Decision Making* In which of the Middle Colonies would you have most liked to live? Explain your thinking. Use the decision-making steps on page H3 of your textbook.

_____

_____

Lesson 1: Working and Trading

Vocabulary

apprentice someone who learns a skill by working for an experienced person

artisan a worker skilled at making things by hand

triangular trade routes trade routes that are between three regions; they make the shape of a triangle

Middle Passage the middle part of a slave's journey from Africa to the Americas

Life for Young Workers

Many young people in the colonies were **apprentices.** Apprentices learned skills from experienced workers, such as rope makers and carpenters. These skills could help them make money as **artisans.** Artisans are workers who make things by hand. Apprentices had to work very long hours. They had little free time. Not all young people were apprentices. Many worked on farms. Others made soap, candles, and other products for their homes.

Colonial Economies

The colonial areas had different economies. The New England economy depended on fishing and timber. The economy of the Middle Colonies was based on farming and minerals such as iron. The Middle Colonies were called "the breadbasket of the colonies" because they grew so much wheat. The Southern Colonies had an economy based on farming. Farms ranged in size from small family farms to large plantations. Cash crops included tobacco, rice, and indigo.

Colonial Trade Routes

The slave trade was very important to the colonial economy. Colonial ships used **triangular trade routes,** or routes shaped like triangles, to trade goods for slaves. On a common triangular trade route, ships sailed from the colonies. The ships brought guns and other goods to West Africa. These things were traded for captured Africans. Then the ships brought the Africans to the West Indies. This part of the trip is known as the **Middle Passage.** Many Africans died on this long and hard journey. The Africans were traded for sugar and molasses in the West Indies. Then ships brought the goods to the colonies. This finished the triangle.

Lesson 1: Review

1. ↻ **Compare and Contrast** Complete the diagram comparing and contrasting the economies of two different colonial areas.

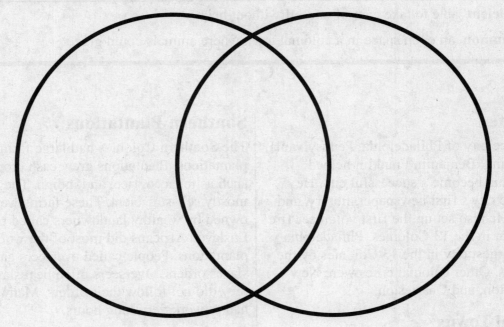

2. Explain the hardships and benefits of working as an apprentice.

_____

_____

3. Which region was known as "the breadbasket of the colonies"? Why?

_____

_____

4. Describe a common triangular trade route. Where did the ships sail? What did they carry from each port?

_____

_____

5. **Critical Thinking:** *Make Decisions* Think about all the types of work described in this lesson. If you were a colonist, which would you most like to do? Explain.

_____

_____

Lesson 2: Cities, Towns, and Farms

Vocabulary

self-sufficient able to take care of oneself without help

town common an open space in a colonial town where animals could graze

City Life

In 1723 the city of Philadelphia, Pennsylvania, was growing. Benjamin Franklin helped Philadelphia become a successful city. He started the city's first newspaper, library, and hospital. He also set up the first volunteer fire department in the 13 Colonies. Philadelphia was the largest city in the 13 Colonies by the mid-1700s. Other colonial cities were New York, Boston, and Charleston.

Colonial Towns

Small towns were set up in New England and the Middle Colonies. Many towns in New England were **self-sufficient.** This means that the towns provided most of their own food and services. Food was grown in fields surrounding the town. Families living in the town owned small plots of land. They grew crops and raised animals on this land. The towns were built around a **town common,** or open grassy area where sheep and cattle could graze. Blacksmiths, coopers, shoemakers, and other workers often had workshops around the town common. The most important building in New England towns usually was the meeting house, where town meetings were held. Many towns in the Middle Colonies were busy marketplaces. Farmers sold crops in these marketplaces. They also came to buy clothing and tools. Most New England and Middle Colony towns had workshops and mills.

Southern Plantations

The Southern Colonies had large farms called plantations. Plantations grew cash crops such as tobacco, rice, and indigo. They were mostly self-sufficient. These farms were owned by wealthy landowners called planters. Enslaved Africans did most of the work on the plantations. People called overseers gave the slaves orders. Overseers often beat slaves if they did not follow their orders. Many slaves had to work very long hours.

Farming Families

Most colonists lived on small family farms. Farming families worked very hard. They made or grew most of what they needed.

Name _____ Date _____

Lesson 2: Review

1. **⟳ Compare and Contrast** Complete the diagram comparing and contrasting a Middle Colony town and a Southern plantation.

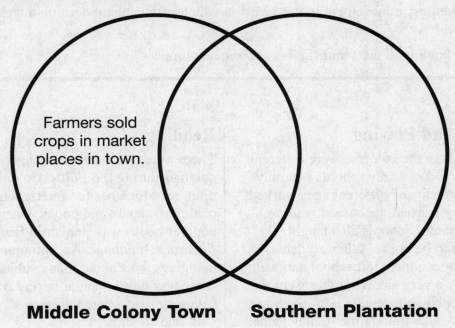

Farmers sold crops in market places in town.

Middle Colony Town   **Southern Plantation**

2. What are some ways that Benjamin Franklin helped improve life for people in Philadelphia?

_____

_____

3. **Critical Thinking: *Evaluate*** You know that New England towns were often built according to a careful design. Do you think this design helped the towns to become self-sufficient? Explain.

_____

_____

4. What types of crops were grown on plantations in the Southern Colonies?

_____

_____

5. Suppose you lived during colonial times. What are four different kinds of places you could live? Which would you choose?

_____

_____

Lesson 3: Everyday Life in the Colonies

Vocabulary

Great Awakening a movement in the 1730s in which people again became interested in religion

almanac a book with facts and figures about many topics

Studying and Playing

Public schools in the colonies were different from schools today. Many schools had only one room. Students of different ages worked together. They learned the basics: reading, writing, and math. Schools also taught students how to be polite. When students became teenagers, most left school and went to work. Only a very small number went to college. Colonial children did a lot of chores at home. They also found time to play games and sports.

Religion in the Colonies

Many different religious groups lived in the colonies. In Europe many people were treated badly because of their religious beliefs. Some colonies were safe places people could run to if they were treated badly. Many colonies were set up as places where people could practice their religion freely. Protestants began the **Great Awakening** in the 1730s. This movement got many colonists interested in religion again. Preachers traveled around and gave fiery speeches. George Whitefield was a leader of the Great Awakening. He collected money to build an orphanage.

Reading

There were dozens of newspapers in the colonies during the 1770s. Colonial families often read together for entertainment. They read newspapers and books. One of the most popular books was Benjamin Franklin's *Poor Richard's Almanack*. An **almanac** is a book that gives facts about many subjects. Only the Bible was more popular during colonial times. Colonists also wrote letters to stay in touch with one another.

Colonial Meals

Corn was used to make many foods. Colonists used it to make bread, pudding, and pancakes. They also made stews made of meat or fish and vegetables. Colonists also ate ice cream, donuts, and fruit pies.

© Scott Foresman 5

Lesson 3: Review

1. ↻ **Compare and Contrast** Complete the diagram comparing and contrasting school in colonial times with school today.

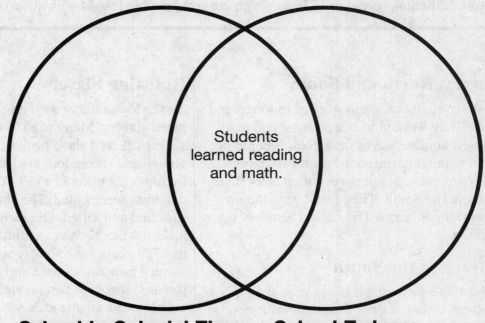

School in Colonial Times   School Today

Students learned reading and math.

2. How were schools in colonial times different from schools today?

_____

_____

3. **Critical Thinking:** *Cause and Effect* Why were some of the English colonies home to people of many different religions?

_____

_____

4. What was the only book in the colonies that sold more copies than *Poor Richard's Almanack* during the mid-1700s?

_____

_____

5. Describe some common meals that a colonial family might enjoy.

_____

_____

© Scott Foresman 5

Lesson 4: Slavery in the Colonies

Vocabulary

Stono Rebellion event in 1739 in which enslaved people fought with slave owners

Slavery, North and South

Most slaves in the North worked in towns and cities. They worked in stores, inns, and in people's homes. Slaves in the North could not travel without permission. Yet these slaves had more chances to improve their lives than slaves in the South. They could earn money by working at night. They could also buy their freedom.

Slavery in the South

In the 1700s the number of slaves in the Southern Colonies grew quickly. This region had more slaves there than in other parts of the colonies. Most slaves in the Southern Colonies worked on plantations. Most enslaved people were taken from West Africa. They brought many skills to the colonies. Some could grow rice. Others were expert carpenters, blacksmiths, or tailors. Slaves had to work very long hours. Their families were often split apart. Many slaves kept African culture alive on the plantations. Family members got together whenever they could. They made musical instruments like those in Africa.

Resisting Slavery

Slaves found many ways to show that they hated slavery. Many tried to escape. Some slaves attacked slave owners. In the **Stono Rebellion,** slaves fought against slave owners in South Carolina in 1739. About 25 white colonists were killed. The slaves were then captured and killed. Olaudah Equiano became a slave when he was a child. He wrote a book in 1789 about how slavery was wrong. Of slavery Equiano said, "Surely this . . . violates [breaks] that first natural right of mankind, equality and independency."

Name _____ Date _____

Lesson 4: Review

1. **Compare and Contrast** Complete the diagram comparing and contrasting slavery in the different regions of the colonies.

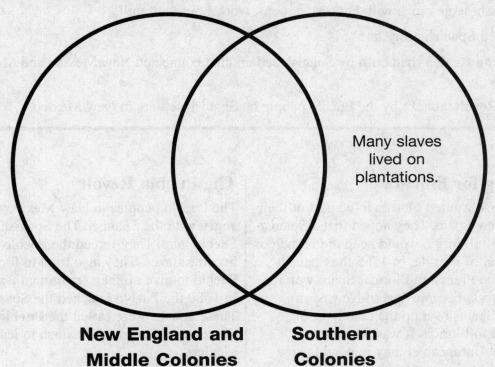

Many slaves lived on plantations.

New England and Middle Colonies   **Southern Colonies**

2. In which region of the 13 Colonies did slavery expand most rapidly during the 1700s?

_____

_____

3. How were enslaved Africans able to keep their traditions alive on plantations?

_____

_____

4. What happened during the Stono Rebellion?

_____

_____

5. **Critical Thinking:** *Analyze Primary Sources* Based on the quote by Olaudah Equiano on page 227, how would you describe his opinion of slavery?

_____

_____

Lesson 1: The Spanish Move North

Vocabulary

hacienda a large ranch with houses, gardens, workshops, and mills

presidio a Spanish army fort

El Camino Real a road built by Spanish settlers that connected New Mexico and Mexico City

Pueblo Revolt attacks by the Pueblo people on Spanish settlers in New Mexico

Fighting for Florida

The Spanish wanted Florida to be part of their colony, New Spain. They hoped that a Spanish settlement in Florida would keep the French or English out of Florida. In 1565 the Spanish attacked the French in Florida. Spain won the battle. Florida became part of New Spain. Then the Spanish set up the colony of St. Augustine in Florida. It was the first permanent European colony in what is now the United States.

New Mexico

The Spanish began to settle in the Southwest. In 1598 the Spanish entered an area they called New Mexico. The Pueblo, Apache, and Navajo peoples had been living on this land. The Spanish were looking for gold and silver in New Mexico. They did not find much. The area was too hot and dry for farming. However, the grasslands were good for ranching. The Spanish set up **haciendas,** or large ranches, to raise sheep and cattle. The Spanish also set up missions in the area. They wanted the Native Americans to become Christians. They built **presidios,** or forts, to protect their missions. They also built a road to connect New Mexico to Mexico City. It was called **El Camino Real.**

The Pueblo Revolt

The Pueblo peoples in New Mexico were angry with the Spanish. The Spanish took over Pueblo land. They forced the Pueblo to become slaves. They also tried to force the Pueblo to give up their traditional ways of life. In 1680 the Pueblo attacked the Spanish. These attacks were called the **Pueblo Revolt.** The Pueblo forced the Spanish to leave New Mexico.

The Spanish Return

The Spanish took over New Mexico again in 1692. They also moved into what is now Texas and Arizona. The Spanish founded the town of San Antonio, Texas, in 1718. The Spanish wanted to keep control over the Southwest. The colony of New Spain grew in the 1700s.

Lesson 1: Review

1. ↻ **Compare and Contrast** Complete the chart by comparing Spanish attempts to begin colonies in different regions of North America.

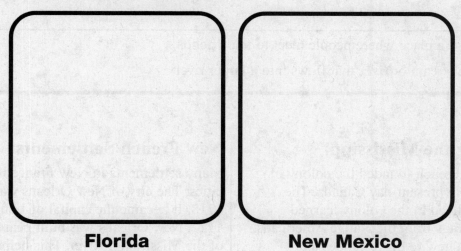

Florida   **New Mexico**

2. Why did the Spanish want to build a colony in Florida?

_____

_____

3. **Critical Thinking:** *Make Inferences* Did the geography of New Mexico influence the economic activities of Spanish settlers in this region? Explain.

_____

_____

4. Explain the purpose of missions in New Spain.

_____

_____

5. Describe three causes of the Pueblo Revolt.

_____

_____

© Scott Foresman 5

Lesson 2: French Explore the Mississippi

Vocabulary

trading post a place where people meet to trade goods

tributary a stream or river that flows into a larger river

Exploring the Mississippi

In 1534, the French founded the colony of New France in present-day Canada. The French who lived in the colony learned important things from the Native Americans. They learned how to make canoes and snowshoes. They traded goods with the Native Americans at **trading posts.** The French also learned of the Mississippi River from Native Americans. The French wanted to control the river. They thought it might help them reach new lands. They could set up more trading posts on these lands. They hoped the river might flow to the Pacific Ocean. Jacques Marquette and Louis Jolliet were French explorers. They explored the Mississippi in 1673. They realized that the river did not flow to the Pacific Ocean.

Founding Louisiana

Robert La Salle was a French explorer. In the 1680s he traveled to the mouth of the Mississippi River. Then La Salle claimed the entire Mississippi River valley for France. He also claimed the river's **tributaries.** Tributaries are streams or rivers that flow into larger rivers. He named the area Louisiana. It became part of New France.

New French Settlements

Many settlements in New France became large cities. The city of New Orleans was set up in 1718. It became the capital of Louisiana in 1722. New Orleans was built near the mouth of the Mississippi River. This helped it become a busy trading center.

Lesson 2: Review

1. **Sequence** Fill in the sequencing chart by putting the lesson's events in correct order.

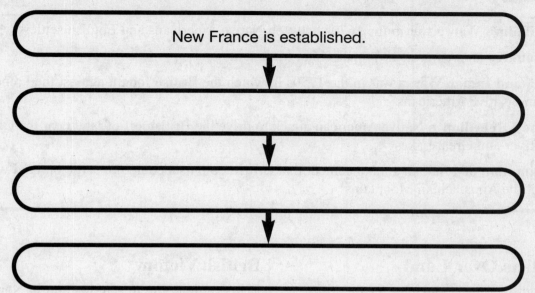

New France is established.

2. How did French settlers first learn about the Mississippi River?

_____

_____

3. **Critical Thinking:** *Point of View* Give two reasons the French were interested in exploring the Mississippi.

_____

_____

4. What did La Salle do when he reached the mouth of the Mississippi?

_____

_____

5. How did New Orleans's location help the city grow?

_____

_____

© Scott Foresman 5

Lesson 3: The French and Indian War

Vocabulary

King Philip's War a war in the 1670s between Native Americans and English settlers

backcountry an area near the Appalachian Mountains

French and Indian War a war in the 1750s in which the British fought against the French and Native Americans

Pontiac's Rebellion a Native American attack to drive the British off of land near the Ohio River and Great Lakes

Proclamation of 1763 an announcement that British colonists could not settle on land west of the Appalachian Mountains

Conflicts Over Land

The English, French, and Native Americans fought to control parts of North America. **King Philip's War** began in New England in 1675. This war was between Native Americans and the English settlers who wanted their land. The English won control over most of New England. In the 1700s some English families moved to the **backcountry.** This was land near the Appalachian Mountains. The English also claimed the Ohio River valley. The Native Americans and the French also wanted this land.

The Ohio River Valley

France would not leave the Ohio River valley. England also wanted this land. England was now called Great Britain. George Washington was an officer in the British army. In 1754 Washington and his soldiers went to build a fort on the Ohio River. Washington decided to take over Fort Duquesne from the French.

The French and Indian War

The **French and Indian War** began in 1754. In this war the British fought against the French and Native Americans friendly with the French. Britain asked a Native American group called the Iroquois League to help them fight the French. The Iroquois refused. Britain was losing the war.

British Victory

British soldiers were sent to fight in North America. The Iroquois also agreed to fight for the British. This helped Britain win the war. The war ended in 1763. Britain took over most of New France. Britain now controlled a lot of Native American land. British settlers began moving onto this land.

Pontiac's Rebellion

Pontiac was a Native American leader. He was angry that the British were settling on his people's land. Pontiac led an attack on the British settlers. This attack is called **Pontiac's Rebellion.** Then King George III made the **Proclamation of 1763.** It said that colonists could not settle on land west of the Appalachian Mountains. Many colonists were upset at the British government. They wanted to settle these lands.

Lesson 3: Review

1. What are the causes and effects of the French and Indian War?

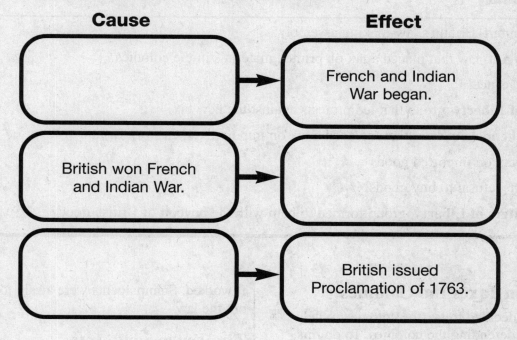

Cause

British won French and Indian War.

Effect

French and Indian War began.

British issued Proclamation of 1763.

2. What factors led to conflicts between the British and the Native Americans?

_____

_____

3. Where and when did the French and Indian War begin?

_____

_____

4. What factors helped the British begin winning battles in the late 1750s?

_____

_____

5. **Critical Thinking:** *Evaluate* Why did the outcome of the French and Indian War lead to new conflicts between British settlers and Native Americans?

_____

_____

Lesson 1: Trouble over Taxes

Vocabulary

Parliament Britain's law-making assembly

Stamp Act law that placed a tax on printed materials in the colonies

repeal cancel

Sons of Liberty group that led protests against the new tax

Townshend Acts laws that replaced a tax on imported goods from Britain

tariff tax on imported goods

boycott refusal to buy goods

Daughters of Liberty group formed to help with the boycott of British goods

Britain Taxes the Colonies

Britain decided to tax the colonies to help pay for defending the colonies. To do this, **Parliament,** the law-making assembly in Britain, passed the **Stamp Act** in 1765. The Stamp Act placed a tax on anything printed in the colonies. This tax made the colonists angry. The colonists had not voted for Parliament. Therefore they felt Parliament had no right to tax them. The colonists felt that they should not be taxed by a government that did not represent, or speak for, them.

Colonists Protest

Patrick Henry was one of the first colonists to speak out against the Stamp Act. He urged others to stand up against the new tax. A meeting called the Stamp Act Congress was held in New York City in October of 1765. Leaders from nine colonies tried to make Parliament **repeal,** or cancel, the Stamp Act.

Sons of Liberty

Samuel Adams formed a group called the **Sons of Liberty.** The Sons of Liberty protested against the new tax. These groups appeared in towns all through the colonies. The groups burned stamps. They frightened stamp agents.

It worked. Stamp agents were afraid to carry out the law.

The Townshend Acts

Parliament voted to end the Stamp Act in 1766. But Britain still needed money. The **Townshend Acts** were passed in 1767. These laws placed a **tariff** on goods such as paper, wool, and tea imported from Britain. Colonists decided to **boycott** these goods. They refused to buy British products.

Women Join the Boycott

A new group called the **Daughters of Liberty** was started to help with the boycott. Daughters of Liberty began weaving cloth that could be used instead of wool from Britain. They used herbs and berries to make tea. The boycott hurt British business. In 1768 British warships arrived in Boston Harbor in hopes of stopping the protests.

© Scott Foresman 5

Lesson 1: Review

1. **Cause and Effect** Fill in the missing causes of the major events from this lesson.

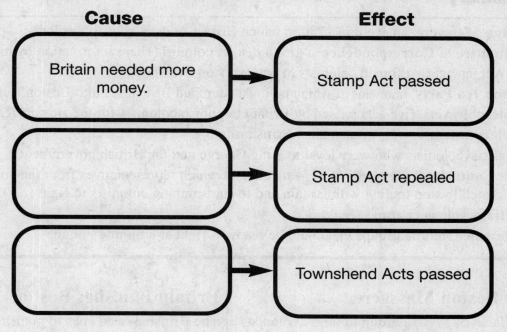

Cause	Effect
Britain needed more money.	Stamp Act passed
	Stamp Act repealed
	Townshend Acts passed

2. What was the Stamp Act?

_____

_____

3. Who were the Sons of Liberty and Daughters of Liberty?

_____

_____

4. How did the British taxes lead to greater cooperation among the colonies?

_____

_____

5. **Critical Thinking:** *Evaluate* Were the colonists' protests successful? Explain your answer.

_____

_____

Lesson 2: The Colonists Rebel

Vocabulary

Boston Massacre an event in 1770 in which British soldiers shot five colonists

Committee of Correspondence a group that let colonists share information by mail

Tea Act an act that forced colonists to pay taxes on British tea

Boston Tea Party an event in which colonists dumped British tea into Boston Harbor

Intolerable Acts five acts passed by Britain to punish colonists for the Boston Tea Party

Patriots colonists who were against British rule

Loyalists colonists who were loyal to King George and the British government

First Continental Congress a 1774 meeting at which representatives from the colonies voted to stop trading with Britain and to start training colonists to fight

militia a volunteer army

minutemen militia groups that could be ready to fight at a minute's notice

The Boston Massacre

On March 5, 1770, a group of angry colonists surrounded some British soldiers in Boston. The soldiers were frightened and fired into the crowd. They killed five people. This event is known as the **Boston Massacre.**

The Committees of Correspondence

The colonies needed a way to share news so they could work together. Samuel Adams formed the first **Committee of Correspondence** in Boston in 1772. Soon other colonies had these committees. Members wrote letters to each other about local events. These letters were carried by "express riders."

The Boston Tea Party

Parliament passed the **Tea Act** to force the colonists to pay a tax on tea. The act also said that the East India Company was the only company allowed to sell tea to the colonies. Colonists did not agree with the act. They said they would not let British ships unload tea in any colonial ports. On December 16, 1773, members of the Sons of Liberty went onto three ships filled with tea. They dumped the tea into Boston Harbor. This event is called the **Boston Tea Party.**

Britain Punishes Boston

The British passed laws to punish the people of Boston for the Boston Tea Party. British soldiers returned to Boston. The colonists had to feed and house the soldiers. A British general was put in control of Massachusetts. Also, the British closed Boston Harbor until the people paid for the ruined tea. Colonists called these laws the **Intolerable Acts.** Colonists became **Patriots** or **Loyalists.** Patriots were against British rule. Loyalists supported British rule.

The Continental Congress

The **First Continental Congress** met in Philadelphia in September 1774. Leaders from most colonies decided to stop trade with Britain until the Intolerable Acts were repealed. They also decided that all colonies should train **militias.** Some militias called themselves **minutemen.** They could be ready to fight at a minute's notice.

Liberty or Death

Patrick Henry made a famous speech in Richmond, Virginia, in March 1775. He warned militias that there was going to be a war between Britain and the colonies.

Lesson 2: Review

1. ⟳ **Cause and Effect** Fill in the missing effects.

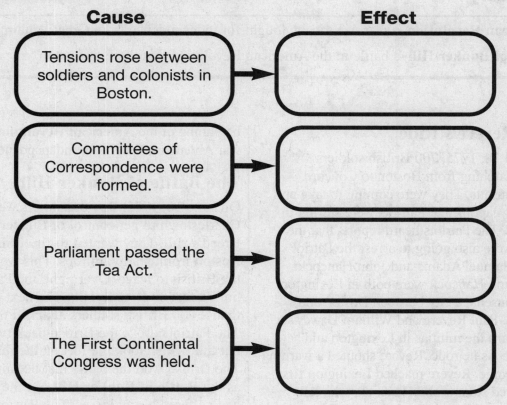

Cause	Effect
Tensions rose between soldiers and colonists in Boston.	
Committees of Correspondence were formed.	
Parliament passed the Tea Act.	
The First Continental Congress was held.	

2. What was the goal of the Committees of Correspondence?

_____

_____

3. What were the Intolerable Acts?

_____

_____

4. What events in Boston helped bring Britain and the colonies closer to war?

_____

_____

5. **Critical Thinking:** *Decision-Making* If you had been a colonist in 1773, would you have been a Patriot or a Loyalist? Use the decision-making steps on page H3 of your textbook.

_____

_____

Lesson 3: The Revolution Begins

Vocabulary

American Revolution a war Americans fought for independence from Great Britain

Battle of Bunker Hill a battle in the American Revolution that the British won

Paul Revere's Ride

On April 18, 1775, 700 British soldiers began marching from Boston to Concord, Massachusetts. They were coming to take and destroy weapons that Patriots were storing in Concord. The Patriots heard reports that the British were also going to arrest the Patriot leaders Samuel Adams and John Hancock. Adams and Hancock were both in Lexington, Massachusetts, a city between Boston and Concord. Paul Revere and William Dawes set out to warn the militias in Lexington and Concord. As he rode, Revere shouted a warning to the people. Revere reached Lexington first. He warned Adams and Hancock, who left before the soldiers arrived. Revere, Dawes, and Dr. Samuel Prescott then rode to Concord but were stopped by British soldiers. Revere was captured, but Dawes got away. Prescott also was able to get away. He completed the ride to Concord to warn the colonists.

The Shot Heard Round the World

On April 19, 1775, the Lexington militia prepared for battle. British soldiers marched into Lexington and faced the colonists. A shot was fired. The British won the battle that followed. Eight colonists were killed and nine were wounded. Only one British soldier had been injured. The British then marched on to Concord. When they reached Concord, they were outnumbered by the militias already there. After a short battle, the British returned to Boston. The Patriots fired on the British as they marched back to Boston and killed or injured 250 British soldiers. These battles marked the beginning of the **American Revolution,** the war Americans fought for independence.

The Battle of Bunker Hill

On June 16, 1775, Patriot soldiers went to Charlestown to get control of Bunker Hill and Breed's Hill. They wanted to fire cannons into Boston from nearby hilltops. This would force the British to leave. Overnight, the Patriots built a fort on Breed's Hill. The next day, more than 2,000 British soldiers attacked the fort. The Patriots drove the British back two times, but the British took the fort on the third attack. The British won the battle that became known as the **Battle of Bunker Hill.** Yet the British had suffered heavy losses. The Patriots were proud of the way they had fought against the British Army.

Lesson 3: Review

1. 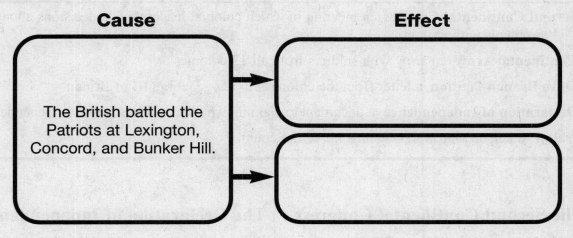 **Cause and Effect** Fill in the two missing effects of the first battles of the American Revolution.

Cause

The British battled the Patriots at Lexington, Concord, and Bunker Hill.

Effect

2. How did Paul Revere warn the colonists that the British were coming?

_____

_____

_____

3. What happened at the Battle of Lexington?

_____

_____

_____

4. What events marked the beginning of the American Revolution?

_____

_____

_____

5. **Critical Thinking:** *Fact or Opinion* Before the Revolution began, one British leader said, "the very sound of cannons" would cause Patriots to run away "as fast as their feet will carry them." Was this a fact or an opinion? How can you tell?

_____

_____

_____

Lesson 1: Declaring Independence

Vocabulary

Second Continental Congress a meeting in which colonial leaders made decisions about problems with Britain

Continental Army an army with soldiers from all 13 colonies

Olive Branch Petition a letter from the colonists to King George III of Britain

Declaration of Independence a document explaining why the colonies wanted independence

traitor a person who works against his or her country

The Second Continental Congress

The **Second Continental Congress** began meeting in Philadelphia in May 1775. The Congress formed the **Continental Army** with soldiers from all 13 colonies. George Washington was elected to lead the Continental Army. The Congress sent King George III a letter called the **Olive Branch Petition.** The letter said that the colonists were still loyal to Great Britain. They did not want to fight a war. The Congress asked the king to give the colonists more self-government. The king said that he would use force to end the rebellion.

"Time to Part"

Thomas Paine was a colonist. In 1776 he wrote a pamphlet called *Common Sense.* The pamphlet convinced many Americans to support the colonies' independence from Britain. The Continental Congress wanted to make sure every colony supported independence. It set up a group to put together the **Declaration of Independence.** The Declaration of Independence explained why the colonies wanted independence. Benjamin Franklin, John Adams, Roger Sherman, Robert Livingston, and Thomas Jefferson decided what would be in the Declaration of Independence. Then Thomas Jefferson wrote the Declaration of Independence.

The Declaration of Independence

In the Declaration of Independence, Thomas Jefferson wrote that people are born with rights that cannot be taken away. These are the right to live, to be free, and to seek happiness. He also wrote that if a government tries to take away these rights, the people have the right to form a new government. The Declaration listed the ways Britain tried to take away colonists' rights. For example, it said that Britain taxed the colonists without their consent. This list showed that the king had abused the colonists' rights. Therefore, the colonists had the right to declare independence and form a new government. Those who signed the Declaration promised to defend the new nation.

A Dangerous Decision

The Declaration of Independence was approved by the Second Continental Congress on July 4, 1776. In August members of the Congress signed the Declaration. They knew it would be dangerous to sign it. The British government would think they were **traitors.** Traitors are people who work against their country.

© Scott Foresman 5

Quick Study

Lesson 1: Review

1. ⟳ **Cause and Effect** Fill in the missing effects of the major events from this lesson.

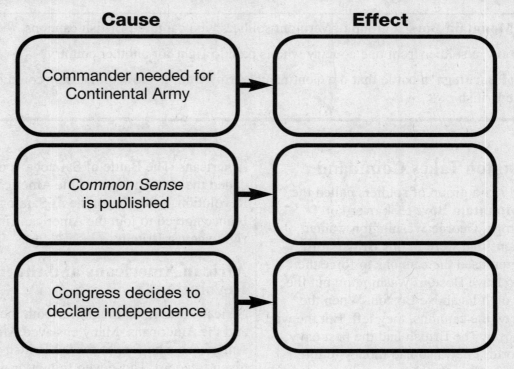

Cause   **Effect**

Commander needed for Continental Army →

Common Sense is published →

Congress decides to declare independence →

2. Describe two important decisions made by the Continental Congress.

_____

_____

3. How did Thomas Paine's *Common Sense* help lead to the Declaration of Independence?

_____

_____

4. Describe Thomas Jefferson's role in creating the Declaration of Independence.

_____

_____

5. **Critical Thinking:** *Express Ideas* Do you think it took courage to sign the Declaration of Independence? Why or why not?

_____

_____

Lesson 2: Patriots at War

Vocabulary

Green Mountain Boys a group of Vermont soldiers who captured British cannons

mercenary a soldier from one country who is paid to fight for another country

Battle of Saratoga a battle that the Continental Army won; it showed that they could defeat the British

Washington Takes Command

In May 1775 a group of soldiers called the **Green Mountain Boys** took over Fort Ticonderoga. George Washington wanted the cannons that were in this British fort. Washington used the cannons to force the British to leave Boston. Washington put the cannons on hills above Boston. When the British saw the cannons, they left. But the war was not over. The British had the best navy in the world. They also had money to hire German **mercenaries.** Mercenaries are soldiers from one country who are paid to fight for another country.

Defeat and Victory

The Americans lost several battles after they forced the British out of Boston. George Washington's army camped in Pennsylvania in December 1776. His troops were running out of supplies. Washington decided to attack Trenton, New Jersey. Trenton was held by German mercenaries fighting for the British. Washington and his army crossed the Delaware River on December 25, 1776. They attacked Trenton the next day. They took the town.

The Turning Point

In the spring, the British began attacking. British General John Burgoyne had a plan to win the war. His plan was to divide the United States in half. In late September and early October, the American and British armies fought in the **Battle of Saratoga.** On October 17, 1777, Burgoyne surrendered to the Americans. The Battle of Saratoga is often called the turning point of the American Revolution. After the Battle of Saratoga, France agreed to join the Americans in their fight against Britain.

African Americans and the Revolution

African Americans fought for both the British and the Americans. Many enslaved African Americans who fought for the British were given freedom. Those who fought or worked as spies for the Americans were also given freedom. After the war some African American Patriots worked to end slavery in the United States.

Women in the Revolution

George Washington had a hard time finding soldiers and getting supplies. Women helped the American Revolution by collecting food, raising money, and making clothing for soldiers. Some women cooked for the army. Others took care of wounded soldiers and fixed uniforms. Some women fought alongside the men. Women also wrote letters and poems supporting independence.

Winter at Valley Forge

In late 1777 the British captured Philadelphia. Washington's army camped in Valley Forge, Pennsylvania, for the winter. The army was running out of food, clothing, and other supplies. During the winter at Valley Forge, many soldiers died of hunger, cold, and disease.

© Scott Foresman 5

Name _____ Date _____

Lesson 2: Review

1. **Sequence** Fill in this diagram by listing four major events from this lesson in the correct order.

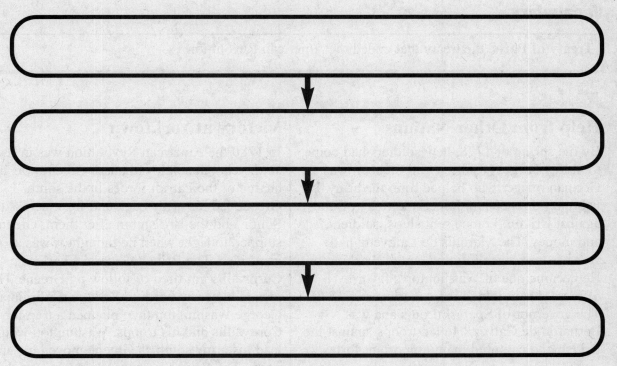

2. How was Washington able to force the British to leave Boston?

_____

_____

3. Describe one important effect of the Battle of Saratoga.

_____

_____

4. **Critical Thinking:** *Fact or Opinion* When the Revolution began, some American leaders did not think African Americans would make good soldiers in the Continental Army. Was this a fact or an opinion? How can you tell?

_____

_____

5. Describe three different ways in which women helped support the American Revolution.

_____

_____

Lesson 3: The World Turned Upside Down

Vocabulary

Treaty of Paris the treaty that ended the American Revolution

Help from Other Nations

By the spring of 1778, new soldiers had come to Valley Forge. Friedrich von Steuben was a German officer who helped train the army. In February, France had joined the war to fight against Britain. France sent ships, soldiers, and money. The Marquis de Lafayette had come from France to join George Washington. He became one of Washington's favorite officers. Spain joined the Americans in 1779. The governor of Spanish Louisiana was Bernardo de Gálvez. He led troops against the British and captured many important forts.

The Fighting Continues

The British Army was unable to defeat the Continental Army in the north. British leaders decided to attack the south. In December 1778 the British Army took Savannah, Georgia. George Rogers Clark led American troops in the west. They took Fort Vincennes in February 1779. The Americans then could control the Ohio River Valley. John Paul Jones was an American captain. In 1779 his ship attacked a British ship. Jones's ship was badly damaged, but he kept fighting. After a long battle, the British surrendered.

Victory at Yorktown

In 1780 the American Revolution was in its sixth year. General Nathanael Greene was in charge of the Patriot forces in the south. Greene led his army back and forth across the South, and the British ran after them. Greene stopped to fight when he thought it was a good idea. The British General Charles Cornwallis got tired of following Greene. He moved his army north to Yorktown, Virginia. George Washington then planned a trap for Cornwallis and his troops. Washington would lead his army south as Greene moved his army north. The French navy blocked Chesapeake Bay so the British could not escape by water. The American forces trapped the British. The British surrendered their entire army on October 19. Yorktown was the last major battle of the American Revolution.

The Treaty of Paris

Americans celebrated the victory at Yorktown. The American Revolution was officially ended when the **Treaty of Paris** was signed in 1783. In the treaty, Britain recognized the United States of America as an independent nation. But the United States now faced new questions. What kind of government would the country have? How long would slavery continue in the United States? What would happen to Native Americans who lived on lands now controlled by the United States?

© Scott Foresman 5

Lesson 3: Review

1. **Draw Conclusions** Complete this diagram by filling in three factors that helped the United States win the American Revolution.

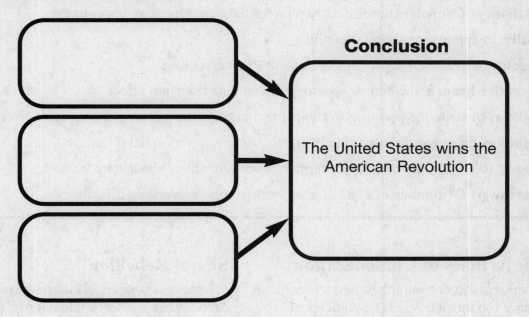

Conclusion

The United States wins the American Revolution

2. Did other nations help the United States win the American Revolution? Explain.

_____

_____

3. What achievements made John Paul Jones a famous Patriot?

_____

_____

4. Explain Washington's strategy for trapping the British at Yorktown.

_____

_____

5. **Critical Thinking:** *Make Predictions* What effect do you think the outcome of the Treaty of Paris will have on Native Americans?

_____

_____

Lesson 1: A Weak Government

Vocabulary

Articles of Confederation an early plan for the new American government

ratify to approve or accept something

legislative branch the part of government that makes laws

executive branch the part of government that puts laws into effect

judicial branch the part of government that makes sure laws are understood correctly

inflation an economic condition in which prices rise very quickly

Shays' Rebellion an uprising of farmers who were angry about state taxes

Northwest Ordinance of 1787 a plan for dividing the Northwest Territory

The Articles of Confederation

Americans did not want their new government to have too much power. The **Articles of Confederation** was a plan for this government. It was **ratified,** or approved, in 1781. It gave states freedom to rule themselves. The Articles said that states would be joined in a league of friendship. The Articles created a weak central government. The central government had only a **legislative branch.** It was called Congress. Congress made laws. Yet it could not collect taxes from the states. The Articles did not set up a **judicial branch,** or court system. They also did not set up an **executive branch** to carry out laws.

A Government in Trouble

The nation did not work well under the Articles of Confederation. The government had to borrow money because it could not collect taxes. The nationalists wanted a stronger central government. The United States also had other money problems. Each state and Congress made its own money. People had trouble figuring the value of the different kinds of money. Prices rose very quickly. This **inflation** made Congress's money almost worthless.

Shays' Rebellion

Massachusetts taxed its citizens to pay back its debts. When farmers could not pay, the state took away their land. Daniel Shays was a farmer in Massachusetts. He led a group of angry farmers in a rebellion. These farmers wanted to close courts that punished people who owed money. They also wanted lower taxes. In 1787 they attacked a government building to get weapons. The attack was not successful. Many nationalists felt **Shays' Rebellion** showed that there should be a stronger central government.

The Northwest Ordinance of 1787

The Treaty of Paris of 1783 gave the United States a lot of land. Congress wanted this land to become states. The Northwest Territory was part of this land. Congress came up with the **Northwest Ordinance of 1787**. It was a plan for dividing the Northwest Territory. It also described how a territory could become a state.

Growing Concerns

Nationalists were getting more worried. George Washington felt that if the states were not joined under a central government the country would be ruined. In May 1787 Congress held a meeting to change the Articles of Confederation.

Lesson 1: Review

1. 🔄 **Draw Conclusions** Fill in the missing facts that lead to the given conclusion.

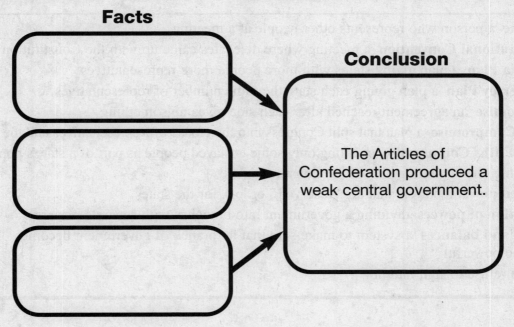

Facts

Conclusion

The Articles of Confederation produced a weak central government.

2. What were the goals of the Articles of Confederation?

_____

_____

3. What caused Shays' Rebellion?

_____

_____

4. **Critical Thinking:** *Cause and Effect* Identify the events that led to the Northwest Ordinance of 1787.

_____

_____

5. What led George Washington to say: "What stronger evidence can be given of the want of energy in our government?"

_____

_____

Lesson 2: Debate in Philadelphia

Vocabulary

delegate a person who represents other people at a meeting

Constitutional Convention a meeting where delegates came up with the Constitution

Virginia Plan a plan giving states with more people more representatives

New Jersey Plan a plan giving each state the same number of representatives

compromise an agreement reached after each side gives up something

Great Compromise a plan that split Congress into the House of Representatives and the Senate

Three-Fifths Compromise counting only some enslaved people as part of a state's population

Preamble the beginning part of the Constitution

reserved powers powers that are "reserved," or left, for the states

separation of powers dividing a government into branches with separate powers

checks and balances a system to make sure that no branch of government becomes too powerful

veto to refuse to sign into law

The Constitutional Convention

In May 1787 **delegates** from the states met. They wanted to change the Articles of Confederation. This meeting was later called the **Constitutional Convention.**

Competing Plans

James Madison and a few other delegates wanted a new constitution. They worked to write the **Virginia Plan.** This plan created executive and judicial branches of government. It gave larger states more delegates in Congress than smaller states. Delegates from smaller states were upset. They came up with the **New Jersey Plan.** This plan gave every state the same number of delegates in Congress.

A Compromise Plan

Delegates finally agreed to a **compromise,** or agreement. They came up with the **Great Compromise.** This plan split Congress into two parts, the Senate and the House of Representatives. In the Senate, every state would have two delegates. In the House of Representatives, states with more people would have more delegates than states with fewer

people. The delegates also agreed to the **Three-Fifths Compromise.** It said that only three out of every five enslaved people could be counted as part of a state's population.

Our Constitution

The **Preamble** tells the Constitution's goals: to protect the country and the people. The Constitution gives some powers to the national government and some to the states. The states' powers are called **reserved powers.** The Constitution divides the country's government into three parts, or branches. Congress makes up the Legislative Branch. The President leads the Executive Branch. The Supreme Court is part of the Judicial Branch. Dividing a government into parts is called a **separation of powers.** The Constitution has a system of **checks and balances.** Even though Congress may pass laws, the President can **veto** a law Congress wants.

The Work Still Ahead

The Constitution was ratified on September 17, 1787. Yet nine of the states still had to agree to it before it could become law.

Lesson 2: Review

1. ⟳ **Draw Conclusions** Add two more facts on which the conclusion given below might be based.

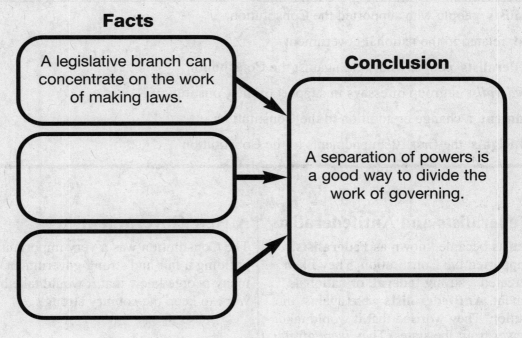

Facts

A legislative branch can concentrate on the work of making laws.

Conclusion

A separation of powers is a good way to divide the work of governing.

2. Did James Madison play an important role in creating the Constitution? Explain.

_____

_____

3. What was the Great Compromise? The Three-Fifths Compromise?

_____

_____

4. What did the delegates to the Constitutional Convention expect to accomplish?

_____

_____

5. **Critical Thinking:** *Evaluate* Why did the writers of the Constitution create a system of checks and balances?

_____

_____

Lesson 3: Ratifying the Constitution

Vocabulary

Federalists people who supported the Constitution

federal related to the national government

Antifederalists people who were against the Constitution

The Federalist a group of essays in support of the Constitution

amendment a change or addition to the Constitution

Bill of Rights the first 10 amendments to the Constitution

The Federalists and Antifederalists

Nationalists became known as **Federalists.** They supported the Constitution. They liked that it created a strong **federal,** or national, government. **Antifederalists** were against the Constitution. They worried that it would take away power from the states. They were afraid that it did not protect the people's rights. They also thought the government would pass laws that were not good for all states. Federalists worked to pass the Constitution. In 1787 they wrote a group of essays called *The Federalist.* The essays argued against the Antifederalist point of view.

The Bill of Rights

A few states quickly ratified the Constitution. Other states were worried that the government would take away the rights of its citizens. The Federalists promised that Congress would add a **Bill of Rights** to the Constitution. The first 10 **amendments,** or changes, to the Constitution became known as the Bill of Rights. They limit the government's power. The Bill of Rights gives certain rights and freedoms to Americans. By 1790 all 13 states accepted the Constitution.

A New Government

The Constitution was a very important step in building a fair and strong government. But many people knew that it would take hard work to keep the country strong.

© Scott Foresman 5

Lesson 3: Review

1. 🔄 **Draw Conclusions** Fill in the diagram with two more facts that support the conclusion.

Facts

Conclusion

Antifederalists argued that the Constitution would reduce the power of the States.	→	
	→	Antifederalists did not want the Constitution to be ratified.
	→	

2. Who were the Federalists? The Antifederalists?

_____

_____

3. What was *The Federalist?*

_____

_____

4. Why is the Bill of Rights so important in American government?

_____

_____

5. **Critical Thinking:** *Express Ideas* Why do you think the Constitution is called a "living document"?

_____

_____

Lesson 1: Washington as President

Vocabulary

electoral college a group of people who vote for President and Vice-President; these people are chosen by each state

inauguration ceremony in which a newly elected President swears loyalty to the Constitution and takes office

Cabinet a group of people who help the President run the country

political party a group of people who share a common view of what government should be and do

President Washington Takes Office

Many important people, such as Thomas Jefferson and Alexander Hamilton, wanted George Washington to become President. On February 4, 1789, he was elected President by the **electoral college.** Each state chose people to be in the electoral college. Washington's **inauguration** was held on April 30. During the ceremony Washington swore his loyalty to the Constitution. President Washington divided the work of the Executive Branch into different departments. The people who led these departments were part of the President's **Cabinet.** President Washington named people to his Cabinet to give him advice and help him run the government.

Political Parties Are Born

Cabinet members had different ideas about how to run the country. Alexander Hamilton believed in a strong national government. Thomas Jefferson did not want a strong national government. Many Americans agreed with each of these men. The sides organized into two **political parties.** Hamilton's party was called the Federalists. Jefferson's party was called the Democratic-Republicans.

A New City

In 1790 the District of Columbia was named the capital of the United States. When George Washington died in 1799, the capital was renamed Washington, D.C. Pierre L'Enfant designed the city. L'Enfant was a French artist and engineer who fought in the American Revolution. A scientist was needed to help plan the city. Benjamin Banneker, a scientist and inventor, was chosen to help.

Living in the President's House

In 1796 John Adams became the second President of the United States. The federal government moved to Washington, D.C., in 1800. Adams and his wife, Abigail, moved into the President's House in 1800. Later, this building would be called the White House. The house and city were not yet finished when President Adams moved in.

© Scott Foresman 5

Lesson 1: Review

1. 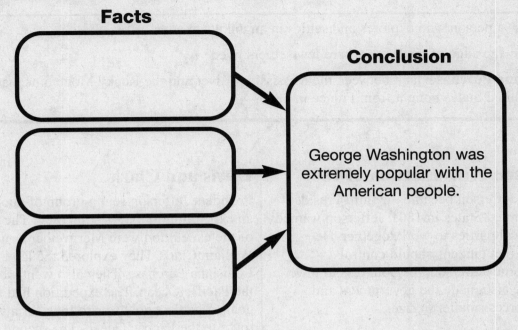 **Draw Conclusions** Fill in the missing facts.

Facts

Conclusion

George Washington was extremely popular with the American people.

2. Explain Washington's purpose in naming people to his Cabinet.

_____

_____

3. **Critical Thinking: *Draw Conclusions*** Why did different political parties emerge in American government?

_____

_____

4. Who were the leaders of the Federalist and Democratic-Republican parties?

_____

_____

5. Why was Benjamin Banneker asked to help design the new capital?

_____

_____

Lesson 2: Jefferson Looks West

Vocabulary

pioneer a person who explores and settles in an unknown area

frontier the edge of the West, where few settlers lived

Louisiana Purchase land between the Mississippi River and the Rocky Mountains that the United States bought from France in 1803

Jefferson Wins Election of 1800

Thomas Jefferson became the third President of the United States in 1801. Jefferson wanted all political parties to work together. He believed that citizens should control government. Jefferson got Congress to lower taxes. He also made the government and armed forces smaller in size.

A Nation Moving West

Americans moved west long before Jefferson was President. These people were called **pioneers.** Daniel Boone was a famous pioneer. He built the Wilderness Road. The Wilderness Road was a trail that helped thousands of pioneers move west of the Appalachian Mountains. Native Americans already lived on this land. Pioneers and Native Americans fought over the land. Pioneers continued to move west. The edge of western settlement was called the **frontier.** The pioneers worked hard to build farms and roads.

The Louisiana Purchase

In 1803 the United States bought an area of land from France. This act was known as the **Louisiana Purchase.** The area was called the Louisiana Territory. It stretched from the Mississippi River to the Rocky Mountains. The purchase doubled the nation's size. It did not cost very much money. The United States bought this land because it wanted to control the city of New Orleans. New Orleans was an important trading port.

Lewis and Clark

President Jefferson sent a group of people on an expedition to the West in 1804. The leaders of the expedition were Meriwether Lewis and William Clark. They explored the land of the Louisiana Purchase. They also went west to the Pacific Ocean. The expedition had three goals. The first goal was to look for a water route to the Pacific Ocean. The second was to meet the Native Americans in the area. The third was to record information about the land, plants, and animals. The team was able to meet the second and third goals. They did not find a water route to the Pacific Ocean.

A Growing Nation

The United States was growing. In 1775 there were two and a half million people. In 1809 there were seven million people. Many new states were formed. Pioneers moved farther and farther west.

© Scott Foresman 5

Lesson 2: Review

1. **Summarize** Fill in the events that are summarized.

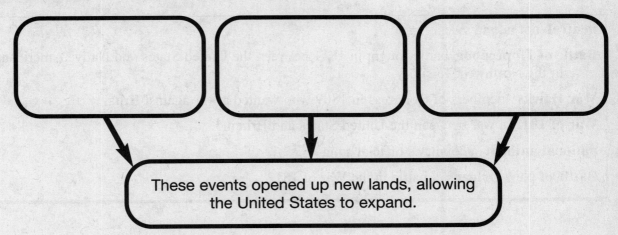

These events opened up new lands, allowing the United States to expand.

2. In your own words, summarize Jefferson's ideas about government.

_____

_____

_____

3. How did Daniel Boone help the pioneers move westward?

_____

_____

_____

4. **Critical Thinking:** *Evaluate* Was the Louisiana Purchase a good deal for the United States? Explain your answer.

_____

_____

_____

5. In what ways did the Lewis and Clark Expedition fulfill its mission?

_____

_____

_____

Lesson 3: Another War with Britain

Vocabulary

neutral not taking sides

Battle of Tippecanoe battle fought in 1811 between the United States and Native Americans in the Northwest Territory

War Hawks members of Congress in 1809 who wanted a war against Britain

War of 1812 a war between the United States and Britain

national anthem a country's official song

Battle of New Orleans a battle in the War of 1812

Moving Toward War

In the early 1800s, Britain and France were at war with each other. Neither country wanted the other to get supplies from the United States. They took sailors and goods from American ships. This action almost stopped trade between the United States and other countries. The United States was angry with Britain. But President Jefferson wanted the country to stay **neutral,** or to not take sides with the British or French. Tecumseh was a Native American leader in the Northwest Territory. Britain supported his attacks on settlers in the area. The United States fought with Tecumseh in the **Battle of Tippecanoe.** Tecumseh did not win. This made him look weak to other Native Americans.

The War of 1812

James Madison became President in 1809. Some members of Congress wanted to go to war with Britain. They were called the **War Hawks.** They wanted to stop Britain's attacks on American ships. They also wanted to end attacks on settlers in the Northwest Territory. The United States declared war on Britain in 1812. This war is called the **War of 1812.** In 1814 British ships tried to pass Fort McHenry in Baltimore, Maryland. The British wanted to invade Baltimore. American forces stopped the British. Francis Scott Key wrote a poem after

watching this battle. Later, music was written for the poem. The song became known as "The Star-Spangled Banner." This song became the **national anthem,** or official song, of the United States.

Battle of New Orleans

British and American forces fought the **Battle of New Orleans.** The United States won. The battle should not have happened because the war was already over. But many Americans did not yet know. The War of 1812 had few effects. Britain and France stopped fighting each other before the War of 1812 ended. They no longer stole from American ships.

© Scott Foresman 5

Lesson 3: Review

1. **Cause and Effect** Fill in each missing cause and effect.

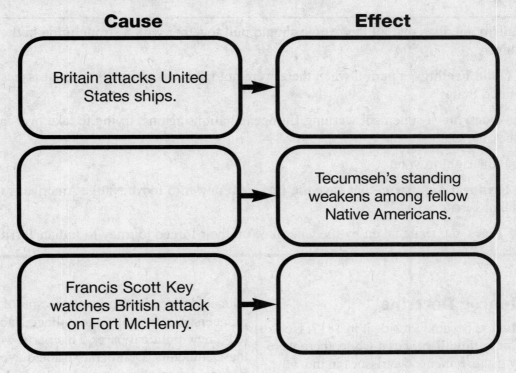

Cause   **Effect**

Britain attacks United States ships.   →   [   ]

[   ]   →   Tecumseh's standing weakens among fellow Native Americans.

Francis Scott Key watches British attack on Fort McHenry.   →   [   ]

2. In what ways did Britain interfere with American shipping on the high seas?

_____

_____

3. **Critical Thinking:** *Make Decisions* If you had been President, would you have gone to war with Britain in 1812? Use the decision-making steps on page H3 of your textbook to explain why or why not.

_____

_____

4. What was produced during the battle of Fort McHenry other than a United States victory?

_____

_____

5. If known, what would have prevented the Battle of New Orleans?

_____

_____

Lesson 1: The United States Turns Fifty

Vocabulary

nationalism the idea that all the people should pull together with a strong pride in their country

Era of Good Feelings a period when there were not many disagreements about issues in the United States

Monroe Doctrine a statement warning European nations against trying to take over land in the Americas

suffrage the right to vote

Indian Removal Act an act that gave the President power to move Native Americans to Indian Territory

Trail of Tears the route taken by the Cherokee on their forced journey to Indian Territory

The Monroe Doctrine

James Monroe became President in 1817. He believed in **nationalism.** For a while, there were not many disagreements over issues in the country. This time was called the **Era of Good Feelings.** Soon there were problems with the Spanish. The Spanish controlled present-day Florida. Many slaves escaped to Florida. Also, Seminole Indians from Florida attacked settlers in Georgia. These settlers had taken over Native American lands. The Spanish did little to stop the attacks. In 1817 the United States attacked the Spanish in Florida. Spain sold Florida to the United States in 1819. Monroe was worried about Russia and Britain taking over parts of Spain's colonies. He put out the **Monroe Doctrine.** It warned European countries against trying to take over land in the Americas.

"The People's President"

In the early 1800s, ideas about society were changing. At first, eastern states gave **suffrage** mainly to white men with property. But the newer states in the west gave all white men the right to vote. By the 1820s a wider range of white men across the United States could vote. Andrew Jackson won the election of 1828. All the Presidents before him were rich and

educated men. Jackson was the son of poor pioneers. He did not go to college. Jackson led a new political party. This party was called the Democrats. Democrats wanted everyone to vote, especially poorer people. Jackson promised equal rights for everyone.

Indian Removal

In the 1820s and 1830s, many Americans moved onto Native American land in the Southeast. President Jackson wanted settlers to move to this land. In 1830 Congress passed the **Indian Removal Act.** The act gave the President power to move Native Americans to Indian Territory. Indian Territory was in present-day Oklahoma. The Cherokee were one of these Native American groups. They tried to keep their land by going to court. The Supreme Court said that the Cherokee had the right to keep their land. President Jackson did not support the Court's decision.

The Trail of Tears

In 1838 the Cherokee were forced to leave their land. The route they took to Indian Territory was known as the **Trail of Tears.** The 800-mile journey was terribly hard. Thousands of Cherokee died along the way.

© Scott Foresman 5

Lesson 1: Review

1. **Compare and Contrast** Fill in the "1830" box to show how conditions in the United States changed from 1817 to 1830.

1817	1830
• James Monroe is President. • Florida belongs to Spain. • American Indians live on land in the southern states.	

2. Why did President Monroe issue the Monroe Doctrine?

_____

_____

3. How did the election of Andrew Jackson as President show that the United States was changing?

_____

_____

4. Why did the United States pass the Indian Removal Act and what was the result?

_____

_____

5. **Critical Thinking:** *Express Ideas* Why is the right to vote important in a democratic society?

_____

_____

Name _____ Date _____

Lesson 2: A New Kind of Revolution

Vocabulary

Industrial Revolution a change in the way goods were produced, from being handmade to being made by machines

manufacture to make goods from raw materials

technology using new ideas to make tools that improve people's lives

cotton gin a machine that cleans seeds out of cotton

mechanical reaper a machine that harvests wheat

canal a ditch dug through the land and filled with water; it usually connects other bodies of water such as rivers, lakes, and seas

The Industrial Revolution

The **Industrial Revolution** changed the way goods were made. Before the Industrial Revolution, goods were made by hand. After the Industrial Revolution, they were made by machine. Machines helped businesses **manufacture** goods cheaper and faster. The Industrial Revolution began in Britain. At first Britain wanted to keep its **technology** a secret. Britain did not want others to know about the new ideas to make tools. The Industrial Revolution came to the United States in the late 1700s. The first cotton-spinning factory was built in New England in 1790. New England factories used rivers to power their machines. Many young girls from nearby farms moved to towns and worked at these factories.

Inventions Change Factories and Farms

Machines that helped businesses make more goods were invented. This meant more products for Americans and for trade. For example, Eli Whitney invented the **cotton gin.** This machine could clean 50 times as much cotton a day as workers could by hand. More cotton could be harvested. This meant that more cloth could be made. The **mechanical reaper** was invented in 1831 by Cyrus McCormick. It helped workers harvest wheat more easily. John Deere came up with a steel plow. It made plowing fields much easier.

Moving Goods and People

People needed better ways to get their products to market. Settlers going west also needed better methods of transportation. The National Road was begun in 1811. It ran from Maryland to Illinois. The road could be rough to travel on. In 1807 Robert Fulton invented a riverboat powered by a steam engine. It made traveling against a river's current much easier. **Canals** were built in areas where there were no rivers. The Erie Canal linked the Great Lakes and the Atlantic Ocean. People and goods could travel on the canal to and from the East and the western frontier.

Early Railroads

On the earliest railroads, horses pulled carts over the rails. The rails were made of wood and covered with iron. In 1830 a steam engine, or locomotive, was built to pull carts over rails. It could pull heavier loads faster than horses could. Railroads became the cheapest and easiest way to travel.

Lesson 2: Review

1. ↻ **Compare and Contrast** Fill in the box to compare the way goods were produced and transported before and after the Industrial Revolution.

Before the Industrial Revolution	After the Industrial Revolution
• Goods were made by hand. • Cotton plants were cleaned by hand. • Wheat was harvested with a long blade. • Goods were moved by horse over rough road.	

2. How did the Industrial Revolution change the way Americans produced goods?

_____

_____

3. Why were New England factory towns built near rivers?

_____

_____

4. **Critical Thinking: *Problem Solving*** Suppose you were an inventor in the early 1830s. What problem would you have wanted to solve? Use the problem-solving steps on page H3 of your textbook.

_____

_____

5. What advantages did the locomotive have over carts pulled along rails by horses?

_____

_____

Lesson 3: The Struggle for Reforms

Vocabulary

reform a change or improvement

revival meeting held to "revive," or bring back and strengthen, people's religious feelings

temperance using only small amounts

abolitionist a reformer who worked to end slavery

Seneca Falls Convention a meeting where women and men talked about the rights women should have

The Second Great Awakening

In the early 1800s, a religious movement, or cause, became popular in the country. It was called the Second Great Awakening. Christian preachers spoke at camp meetings called **revivals.** The purpose of these meetings was to "revive," or bring back, people's religious feelings. This movement caused people to think about religion in their lives. It also brought about a wish for **reform,** or change. Many people wanted to make life better for people around them. They were called reformers. Some reformers tried to get people to stop drinking alcohol. They were part of the **temperance** movement. Other reformers wanted to put an end to slavery. Still others worked to gain rights for women.

Fighting Against Slavery

In the 1830s the movement to end slavery became strong. **Abolitionists** worked to abolish, or erase, slavery. Frederick Douglass escaped slavery. He gave powerful speeches against slavery. William Lloyd Garrison started an abolitionist newspaper. It was called *The Liberator.* Sojourner Truth escaped slavery. She used the Bible in her speeches against slavery. She also spoke about women's rights.

Women's Rights

Women had few rights in the early 1800s. They were not allowed to vote. Married women could not own property. They could not go to most colleges. Elizabeth Cady Stanton and Lucretia Mott worked for women's rights. In 1848 they put together the **Seneca Falls Convention.** At this meeting, women and men talked about the rights women should have.

The Spirit of Reform

Reformers worked to bring about other changes. Horace Mann believed education could help poor people. He set up more high schools in Massachusetts. He also made sure the school year was at least six months long in that state. Dorothea Dix worked to improve conditions in prisons and mental institutions.

Lesson 3: Review

1. 🕐 **Compare and Contrast** Fill in the "Goals" box to compare problems in the United States with goals of reformers.

Problems	Goals
• Slavery • Women did not have equal rights with men.	

2. What reform movements were produced by the Second Great Awakening?

_____

_____

3. What did Frederick Douglass and Sojourner Truth have in common?

_____

_____

4. Compare the rights of men and women in the early 1800s.

_____

_____

5. **Critical Thinking:** *Make Inferences* Why might many reformers have worked for—or at least supported—several different reforms?

_____

_____

Lesson 1: Settling the South and Texas

Vocabulary

Texas Revolution a war between Texas and Mexico for Texas's independence
annex to add a territory to a country or state
manifest destiny the belief that the United States should reach west to the Pacific Ocean
Mexican War a war between the United States and Mexico in the 1840s
Bear Flag Revolt rebellion by California settlers against the Mexican government
Treaty of Guadalupe Hidalgo the treaty that ended the Mexican War

Moving South

Settlers began moving to the new southern frontier in greater numbers after the defeat of the Native Americans. Also, the rich soil and warm climate were ideal for growing cotton, and iron was discovered.

The Story of Texas

During the 1820s Stephen F. Austin brought American settlers to Texas, then part of Mexico. By 1830 Mexico stopped allowing American settlers into Texas for several reasons. Slavery was not allowed in Mexico, yet many settlers brought slaves. Many settlers would not practice the Catholic religion and wanted more say in the government. The Mexicans were afraid that the settlers would revolt. In 1835 the settlers began to fight for independence in the **Texas Revolution.** Although the brave defenders of the Alamo were defeated, Sam Houston led Texans to defeat the Mexicans near the San Jacinto River. They forced Mexican President Santa Anna to move his troops south of the Rio Grande. Texas became an independent country with Houston as president. He asked the United States to **annex** Texas as a state. Some Americans believed in **manifest destiny.** Others were afraid that adding Texas would expand slavery and lead to war with Mexico. President Andrew Jackson chose not to annex Texas. He knew that Americans did not agree about annexing Texas. Texas finally became a state in 1845.

War with Mexico

The **Mexican War** broke out between the United States and Mexico in 1846. Mexico then controlled California. American settlers in California revolted against the Mexican government. This revolt was called the **Bear Flag Revolt.** The settlers declared their independence from Mexico. They fought against Mexico with U.S. troops. In 1847 the United States took control of New Mexico and California. Zachary Taylor was an American general. He won an important battle at Buena Vista in 1847.

New Borders

General Winfield Scott captured Mexico City, Mexico, in 1847. The **Treaty of Guadalupe Hidalgo** ended the war in 1848. Mexico sold most of its northern territory to the United States. Many new states, including California, were later formed out of this land. In 1846 the Oregon Territory Treaty added more land to the United States. In 1853 the Gadsden Purchase added still more land. The United States now stretched from the Atlantic Ocean to the Pacific Ocean.

Mexican Americans

Many Mexicans stayed on the land won by the United States. They showed settlers how to irrigate soil and raise cattle. Also, many Spanish words became part of the English language.

© Scott Foresman 5

Quick Study

Lesson 1: Review

1. ⟳ **Compare and Contrast** Fill in the diagram comparing and contrasting United States boundaries in 1844 and 1854.

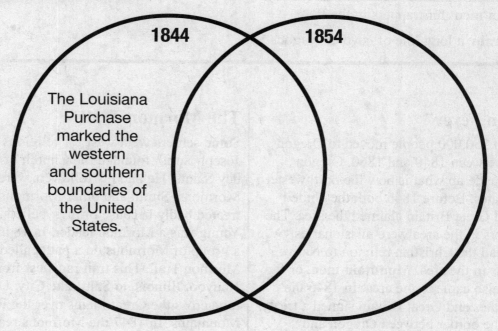

1844   1854

The Louisiana Purchase marked the western and southern boundaries of the United States.

2. What factors attracted settlers to the new Southern frontier?

_____

_____

3. **Critical Thinking:** *Summarize* How did Texas gain its independence from Mexico?

_____

_____

4. Why did President Andrew Jackson refuse Sam Houston's request for the United States to annex Texas?

_____

_____

5. How did Generals Winfield Scott and Zachary Taylor contribute to the United States victory in the Mexican War?

_____

_____

Lesson 2: Trails to the West

Vocabulary

mountain men fur trappers in the West

wagon train a long line of covered wagons

"Oregon Fever"

More than 350,000 people moved to Oregon Country between 1840 and 1860. Oregon Country made up what is now the northwestern United States. Before 1846 both the United States and Great Britain claimed the area. The first settlers in the area were missionaries. They spread the Christian religion to Native Americans in the area. **Mountain men,** or fur trappers, also came to the area. In 1846 the United States and Great Britain signed a treaty. It set up the border between Oregon and Canada. Settlers came to Oregon after this agreement for different reasons. Some came to start new lives.

Settlers traveled 2,000 miles northwest on the Oregon Trail to get to Oregon. They used wagons pulled by oxen or horses. Usually, many people traveled together. They formed a long line of wagons called a **wagon train.** People traveled in groups for protection. Travel was dangerous and hard. Many people died in accidents. People also headed west on other trails. Settlers looking for farmland or gold traveled on the California Trail. It ran from Independence, Missouri, to California. Traders, trappers, and settlers followed the Old Spanish Trail. It ran from Santa Fe, New Mexico, to Los Angeles, California. Silver and fur traders traveled on the Santa Fe Trail. This trail ran from Missouri to Santa Fe, New Mexico.

The Mormon Trail

Some settlers went west for religious freedom. Joseph Smith founded the Church of Latter-day Saints. He and his followers were called Mormons. Smith and other Mormons were treated badly because of their beliefs. Brigham Young was a Mormon leader. In 1846 he led a group of Mormons on a path called the Mormon Trail. This trail ran west from Nauvoo, Illinois, to Salt Lake City, Utah. It ran across the Great Plains over the Rocky Mountains. In 1847 the Mormons reached present-day Utah. The area still belonged to Mexico. They founded Salt Lake City there.

© Scott Foresman 5

Lesson 2: Review

1. **Summarize** Fill in the missing detail and summary of the lesson.

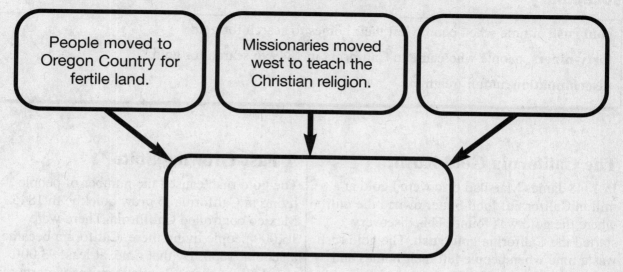

2. What were the advantages and disadvantages of traveling west by wagon train?

_____

_____

_____

3. Write a one-sentence summary describing each of the main trails leading west.

_____

_____

_____

4. Explain the reasons different groups of people moved west.

_____

_____

_____

5. **Critical Thinking: *Draw Conclusions*** Why do you think the 1846 treaty between the United States and Great Britain encouraged more settlement in Oregon Country?

_____

_____

_____

Lesson 3: The Golden State

Vocabulary

gold rush a time when people left their homes to search for gold

forty-niners people who came to California in 1849 to search for gold

discrimination unfair treatment

The California Gold Rush

In 1848 James Marshall discovered gold at a mill in California. John Sutter owned the mill where the gold was found. This discovery started the California **gold rush.** The gold rush was a time when people left their homes and jobs. They came to California to find riches. In 1849 over 80,000 people came to the state. These people were called **forty-niners** because of the year they arrived. Many came from the east by wagon on the California Trail. This trail stretched over the Sierra Nevada mountain range. Others traveled by ship to San Francisco. San Francisco was a small town before the gold rush. In 1847 about 800 people lived there. The gold rush turned San Francisco into a large city. By 1860 the population was about 57,000. To get to San Francisco, people from the east coast sailed around the southern tip of South America. Then they sailed north to California. Some people sailed to the east coast of Central America. Then they walked across Central America to the Pacific Ocean and took boats to California.

Mining for Gold

Most forty-niners found little or no gold. Searching for gold was hard work. Food and supplies cost a lot of money. Many miners left. Some people made a lot of money selling supplies to miners. Levi Strauss came from Germany. He made and sold pants that would not fall apart easily. Many miners found these pants useful.

A Fast-Growing State

The gold rush caused the number of people living in California to grow quickly. In 1845 Mexico controlled California. There were 15,000 people living there. California became a state in 1850. By that time, at least 93,000 people lived there. People from many parts of the world came to California. Many of these people experienced **discrimination,** or unfair treatment. In 1850 the state began taxing miners not born in the United States. Miners born in the United States did not have to pay the tax.

© Scott Foresman 5

Lesson 3: Review

1. 🔄 **Compare and Contrast** Fill in the box to show how California changed after the discovery of gold.

Before Discovery of Gold	After Discovery of Gold
• Population of San Francisco is 800. • California's population is about 17,000. • California is not a state.	

2. Who were the forty-niners and why were they called this name?

_____

_____

3. Describe three routes people from the eastern part of the United States used to travel to California.

_____

_____

4. Do you think the gold-mining life was what the miners expected it to be? Explain.

_____

_____

5. **Critical Thinking:** *Analyze Information* What might lead you to conclude that there was discrimination against immigrants in California in 1850?

_____

_____

Lesson 1: North and South Grow Apart

Vocabulary

sectionalism a loyalty to a section of a country rather than to the whole country

Two Regions

The Southern and Northern parts of the United States became very different from each other. In the South most people lived and worked on farms. Southern towns were usually small. In the North many people moved to big cities to work in factories. Southerners and Northerners had different wants. In 1846 Congress lowered tariffs on goods from other countries. Tariffs are taxes paid on imported goods. Northerners were angry. This would cause people to buy goods from other countries. They would not buy as many goods made in the North. Southerners were happy. They could continue to buy goods from Great Britain cheaply. These differences caused a split between the North and South, or **sectionalism.**

Slavery in the South

By 1850 slavery was illegal in most Northern states. But slavery was allowed in the South. Slavery was very important to the economy of the South. Cotton was a main crop in this area. Most slaves worked in the cotton fields. Slaves worked on plantations and on small farms. As the demand for cotton grew, so did the number of slaves in the South. In 1860 there were almost four million enslaved African Americans in the United States. The number of free African Americans was much lower. Most free African Americans lived in the North. They did not have the same rights as whites.

Different Views on Slavery

Many people were against slavery. They felt that one person should not be allowed to own another. Slave owners in the South felt differently. They argued that factory workers in the North were treated worse than slaves were.

Lesson 1: Review

1. 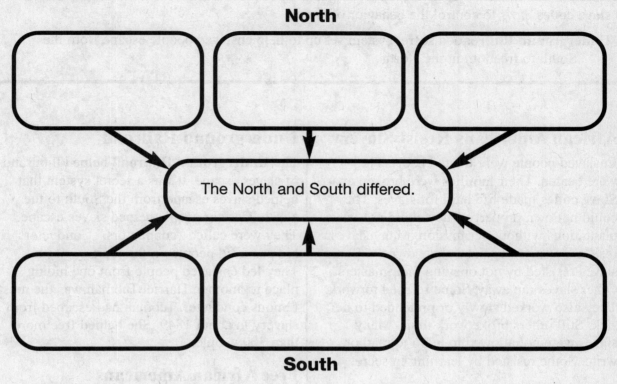 **Main Idea and Details** Complete the graphic organizer to show details supporting the main idea.

North

The North and South differed.

South

2. **Critical Thinking:** *Compare and Contrast* Identify two main differences between life in the North and South.

_____

_____

3. Describe how tariffs affected relations between North and South. Use the word sectionalism in your answer.

_____

_____

4. In 1860 were more African Americans enslaved or free?

_____

_____

5. Describe the main argument of people opposed to slavery.

_____

_____

Lesson 2: Resisting Slavery

Vocabulary

slave codes laws to control the behavior of slaves

Underground Railroad a secret system set up to help enslaved people escape from the South to freedom in the North

African Americans Resist Slavery

Enslaved people were treated badly. They were beaten. Their families were broken apart. **Slave codes** made life hard for slaves. They could not own property. They could not leave plantations without permission. Many slaves resisted, or acted against, slave owners. Some slaves resisted by not obeying their masters. Other slaves ran away. Some refused to work. They also worked slowly or pretended to be sick. Still others broke work tools. Many slaves were not allowed to learn to read or write. Some resisted by learning in secret.

Slave Rebellions

Slave owners worried about rebellions, or battles, against slave owners. They did not allow slaves to hold meetings. Yet some slaves did lead rebellions. Nat Turner was a slave in Virginia. He led a rebellion in 1831. Turner and his followers killed 60 whites. United States and Virginia troops stopped the rebellion. They killed more than 100 African Americans. In 1839 Africans took over a Spanish slave ship that was bringing them to Cuba. The ship was called the *Amistad*. The United States captured the ship. The Africans were taken to prison. The Supreme Court ruled that the Africans should be freed.

Underground Railroad

The **Underground Railroad** helped thousands of slaves escape. It was a secret system that helped slaves escape from the South to the North. Certain people helped slaves escape. They were called "conductors." Conductors hid enslaved people on the journey north. They led enslaved people from one hiding place to another. Harriet Tubman was the most famous conductor. Tubman had escaped from slavery in about 1849. She helped free more than 300 people.

Free African Americans

By 1860 only a small number of African Americans were free. They faced many difficulties. Slave owners could capture escaped slaves in the North. Many Southern states did not let free African Americans work certain jobs. Some white people in the South and North threatened or hurt African Americans who were looking for work. But many free African Americans found jobs and owned property.

Lesson 2: Review

1. 🔄 **Main Idea and Details** Complete the graphic organizer to show the details that support the main idea that enslaved African Americans resisted slavery.

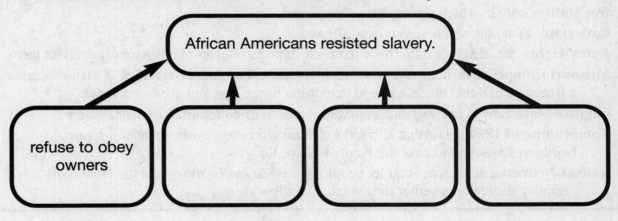

African Americans resisted slavery.

refuse to obey owners

2. Compare and contrast different ways by which African Americans resisted slavery.

_____
_____
_____

3. **Critical Thinking:** *Cause and Effect* What did slave owners do to try to prevent rebellions such as that of Nat Turner and his followers?

_____
_____
_____

4. Describe how enslaved African Americans escaped to freedom on the Underground Railroad.

_____
_____
_____

5. What challenges were faced by free African Americans in the North and South?

_____
_____
_____

Lesson 3: The Struggle Over Slavery

Vocabulary

free state a state in which slavery was not allowed

slave state a state in which slavery was allowed

states' rights the idea that states have the right to make choices about issues that affect them

Missouri Compromise a law that allowed Missouri to become a slave state if Maine became a free state and that made a line to determine future free and slave states

Fugitive Slave Law a law that said runaway slaves must be returned to their owners

Compromise of 1850 a law that allowed California to become a free state; in return, Northern states had to pass the Fugitive Slave Law

Kansas-Nebraska Act an act that let people in the Kansas Territory and the Nebraska Territory decide on whether they wanted to allow slavery

Missouri Compromise

In 1819 there were 11 **free states** and 11 **slave states.** The people of Missouri asked to become a slave state. Southern states agreed with the people of Missouri. Northern states did not. Some Southern leaders believed in **states' rights** and felt that states should decide whether to allow slavery. The **Missouri Compromise** was a solution. Missouri became a slave state, and Maine became a free state. New states north of a line drawn westward would be free states and those south of it could allow slaves.

The Compromise of 1850

California asked to become a free state in 1849. Then there would be more free states than slave states. **The Compromise of 1850** allowed California to become a free state. In return Northern states had to pass the **Fugitive Slave Law.** The compromise also affected people in the territories won from Mexico. These people could vote on whether they wanted to allow slavery.

"Bleeding Kansas"

In 1854 Nebraska was split into two territories— the Nebraska Territory and the Kansas Territory. Congress passed the **Kansas-Nebraska Act.** The people of Kansas voted for slavery. Many voters

were not from Kansas. Northerners claimed the vote was illegal and violence broke out.

A Divided Country

Other events caused a deeper split between the North and South. One was the court case of Dred Scott in 1857. Dred Scott was a slave. He claimed he was free. The Supreme Court ruled that he was not free. The court decided that African Americans had no rights. In 1859 an abolitionist named John Brown tried to lead an attack on slave owners in Virginia. He was caught and hanged.

A New Political Party

Ideas about slavery caused the Whig political party to split apart. Members of the Whigs who were against slavery helped form the Republican Party. Abraham Lincoln was a Republican opposed to the spread of slavery. Yet he did not want the country to go to war over slavery.

Lincoln Is Elected President

Abraham Lincoln was elected President in 1860, but he did not get any Southern electoral votes. Southerners were afraid that Lincoln would end slavery and that their opinions would not matter to the new government.

Lesson 3: Review

1. ⟳ **Main Idea and Details** Complete the graphic organizer to identify the events supporting the main idea of the lesson.

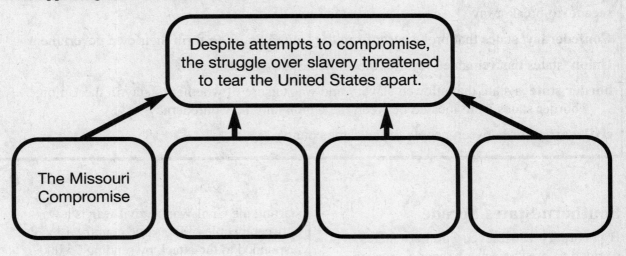

Despite attempts to compromise, the struggle over slavery threatened to tear the United States apart.

The Missouri Compromise

2. How did the Missouri Compromise keep the balance of free and slave states?

_____

_____

3. How did the Compromise of 1850 affect slavery in California and the territories gained from Mexico?

_____

_____

4. Who were Dred Scott and John Brown? How did their actions affect the split between North and South?

_____

_____

5. **Critical Thinking:** *Make Inferences* What was more important to Abraham Lincoln, abolishing slavery or preserving the nation? Explain.

_____

_____

_____

© Scott Foresman 5

Lesson 4: The First Shots Are Fired

Vocabulary

secede to break away

Confederacy states that broke away from the United States to form their own government

Union states that remained loyal to the United States government

border state a state that allowed slavery and was unsure of whether to stay in the Union; border states were located between the Union and the Confederacy

civil war a war between people of the same country

Southern States Secede

By February 1861 seven Southern states decided to break away, or **secede,** from the United States. States that remained loyal to the United States government were called the **Union.** South Carolina, Alabama, Florida, Mississippi, Georgia, Louisiana, and Texas seceded. These states formed their own government called the **Confederacy.** The Confederacy created its own constitution. It supported states' right and slavery. The Confederacy elected Jefferson Davis as its president. Davis was a former U.S. senator from Mississippi. Davis was concerned that the United States would oppose the Confederacy. When Lincoln became president on March 4, 1861, the Confederacy had taken control of most of the military property in the South. One of the forts still under Union control was Fort Sumter in Charleston, South Carolina.

The War Begins

In April 1861 the Confederacy demanded that the Union surrender Fort Sumter. When the fort's commander, Major Robert Anderson, did not immediately surrender, Jefferson Davis ordered Confederate soldiers to attack the fort,

starting the Civil War. A **civil war** is a war between people of the same country. Lincoln responded to the attack by sending 75,000 Union soldiers to put down the Confederate rebellion. Lincoln thought it would take about 90 days. Lincoln's call for troops angered people in Virginia, Arkansas, Tennessee, and North Carolina. These four states then joined the Confederacy. There were now 11 states in the Confederacy and 23 in the Union. Four of the Union states—Delaware, Maryland, Missouri, and Kentucky—were slave states. They weren't sure if they wanted to stay in the Union or join the Confederacy. These were called the **border states,** because they were located between the Union and the Confederacy. Lincoln wanted to keep these slave states in the Union, so he said the main reason for fighting the war was to hold the United States together, not to abolish slavery. Still, some Northerners believed that the main purpose of the war was to end slavery. Southerners fought to preserve states' rights and slavery. Some Southerners referred to the conflict as the War for Southern Independence. The war was also called the War Between the States. The Civil War lasted longer and was bloodier than anyone had expected.

© Scott Foresman 5

Lesson 4: Review

1. ⟳ **Main Idea and Details** Complete the graphic organizer to show the details that support the main idea.

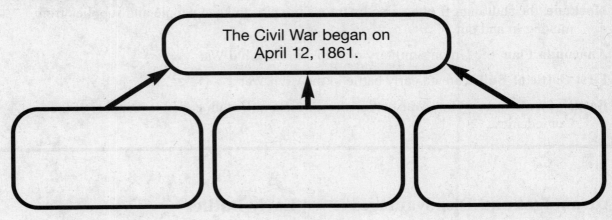

2. Describe two key goals of the Confederate constitution.

_____

_____

_____

3. Identify the event that started the Civil War.

_____

_____

_____

4. Describe Abraham Lincoln's main reason for fighting the Civil War.

_____

_____

_____

5. **Critical Thinking: *Express Ideas*** Why do you think that at the beginning of the Civil War Lincoln did not say that he was fighting the war to end slavery?

_____

_____

_____

Lesson 1: The Early Stages of the War

Vocabulary

blockade the shutting off of an area by troops or ships to keep people and supplies from moving in and out

Anaconda Plan the Union's military plan to win the Civil War

First Battle of Bull Run an early battle in the Civil War

Battle of Antietam a Civil War battle; after Antietam, Britain ended its support of the Confederacy

Advantages and Disadvantages

Many Northerners believed they were fighting the Civil War to keep the United States together. Most Southerners were fighting to keep their way of life. Both sides had advantages. Many Southerners were hunters who were familiar with weapons. The South had a history of producing military leaders. Many Southerners fought in the Mexican War. The North had more weapons and supplies such as cloth, iron, and wheat. The North also had more ways of moving supplies. It had many more railroads, canals, and roads. The North also raised much more money than the South.

Strategies

General Winfield Scott came up with the **Anaconda Plan** to fight the Confederacy. Just as an anaconda snake squeezes its prey, the Union would squeeze the Confederacy to beat them. First, the Union would set up a **blockade** of the Atlantic and Gulf coasts. The blockade would prevent the Confederacy from selling cotton to Britain to make money for the war. It would also cut off supplies to the South. Second, the Union would gain control over the Mississippi River. This would weaken the South by cutting it in half. Third, the Union would attack the Confederacy from the east and west. The Confederacy thought the Union would get tired and give up. It was also counting on Britain to help fight the Union.

Early Battles

In July 1861 Union and Confederate troops fought in the **First Battle of Bull Run.** Early in the battle, there was much confusion. Most of the soldiers had never fought in a war. The South was losing at first. But "Stonewall" Jackson, a Confederate general, and his soldiers would not turn back. More Confederate soldiers arrived. The Confederacy won, but both sides lost thousands of soldiers. In September 1862 the **Battle of Antietam** was fought. The Union won. After Antietam, Britain decided not to help the Confederacy.

Technology and War

People used new technology during the Civil War. New guns shot farther. Railroads moved troops around more easily. Confederate submarines sailed under Union ship blockades. Soldiers also used early versions of the hand grenade. Both sides used iron-covered ships. The *Virginia* was the Confederacy's iron-covered ship. It battled against the Union's iron-covered ship, the *Monitor*. A huge number of soldiers died because of these new weapons. Medical technology had not advanced far enough to save their lives.

© Scott Foresman 5

Lesson 1: Review

1. 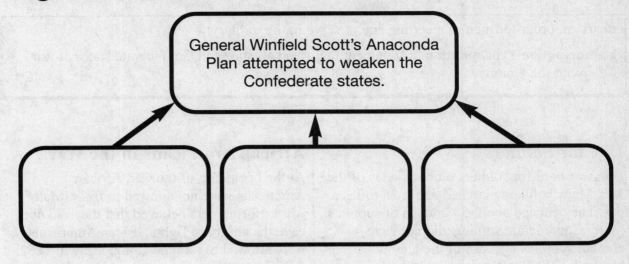 **Main Idea and Details** Fill in the details of the Anaconda Plan.

General Winfield Scott's Anaconda Plan attempted to weaken the Confederate states.

2. Compare advantages the Union had at the beginning of the war to those of the Confederacy.

   _____

   _____

   _____

3. How did the strategies of the North and South differ?

   _____

   _____

   _____

4. Summarize the events of the First Battle of Bull Run.

   _____

   _____

   _____

5. **Critical Thinking:** *Analyze Information* What effect did military technology have on Civil War soldiers?

   _____

   _____

   _____

Lesson 2: Life During the War

Vocabulary

draft an order for men of a certain age to serve in the military

Emancipation Proclamation a statement that freed all slaves in Confederate states at war with the Union

Life for Soldiers

Life was hard for soldiers on both sides of the war. Many soldiers marched about 25 miles a day. They carried about 50 pounds of supplies. Many Confederate soldiers did not have enough supplies because of the Union blockade. The **draft** was passed as a law in the North and the South. The draft made men of a certain age serve in the military. Men in the North could pay $300 to get out of the draft. Southern men who owned 20 or more slaves could pay someone to fight in their place. That is why many called the war "a rich man's war and a poor man's fight." Hundreds of thousands of soldiers died on both sides. Most died from disease rather than in battle.

The Emancipation Proclamation

On January 1, 1863, President Lincoln issued the **Emancipation Proclamation.** This statement freed all slaves in Confederate states at war with the Union. Slaves in Confederate states that were already controlled by the Union were not freed. It also did not free slaves in border states. Lincoln believed that he could save the Union by ending slavery. Frederick Douglass was a free African American. He encouraged African Americans to help fight the Confederacy.

African Americans in the War

At the beginning of the war, African Americans were not allowed to fight. Many white Northerners believed that they did not have the ability to fight. African Americans were allowed to join the Union army in 1862. African Americans were not treated the same as white soldiers. They did not get equal pay. In 1863 the African American Massachusetts 54th Regiment led an attack on Fort Wagner in South Carolina. Many soldiers of this regiment died. But they proved to Northerners that they could fight. By June 1864 Congress gave African American and white soldiers equal pay.

Women and the War

Women on both sides helped the war effort. Some women fought or acted as spies. Many women nursed wounded soldiers. Others became teachers, office workers, or ran farms and businesses while their husbands were fighting. Women on both sides lost loved ones in the war. Women in the South also faced shortages of supplies. This made prices in the South rise very high. But both Northern and Southern women made clothing and other supplies that they sent to the armies. They also sent as much food as they could spare.

The War Goes On

By 1863 soldiers on both sides wanted the war to end. They were tired. Their shelter was poor. Many of their friends and family members had died. Many soldiers left the army without permission.

© Scott Foresman 5

Lesson 2: Review

1. ↻ **Main Idea and Details** Fill in the details that support the main idea.

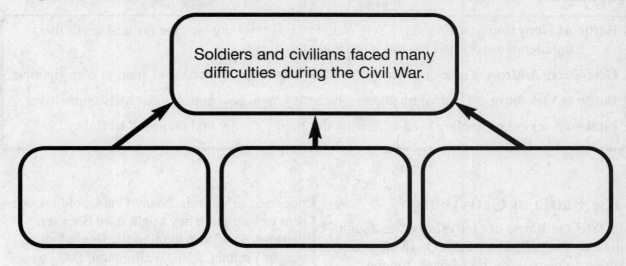

Soldiers and civilians faced many difficulties during the Civil War.

2. Why was the Civil War called a "rich man's war and a poor man's fight"?

_____

_____

3. **Critical Thinking:** *Problem Solving* Suppose you had to help President Lincoln decide when to issue the Emancipation Proclamation. How would you solve this problem? Use the problem-solving steps outlined on page H3 in your book.

_____

_____

4. How did the Massachusetts 54th help the Union?

_____

_____

5. What role did women play in the Civil War?

_____

_____

Lesson 3: How the North Won

Vocabulary

Battle of Gettysburg a three-day Civil War battle; Gettysburg was the farthest north that Confederate forces had pushed into Union territory

Gettysburg Address a speech given by President Lincoln; it inspired the Union to keep fighting

Battle of Vicksburg a Civil War battle in which the Union got control of the Mississippi River

total war a kind of warfare used to destroy the enemy's army and their will to fight

The Battle of Gettysburg

In 1863 the **Battle of Gettysburg** was fought in Gettysburg, Pennsylvania. On the first day, Union soldiers were forced back. On the second day, Union soldiers held their ground on hills. On the third day, both sides exchanged cannon fire. "Pickett's Charge" followed, a mass attack by Confederates across open ground toward well-protected Union troops. The attack was a disaster for the Southern troops and they retreated back into Virginia.

The Gettysburg Address

President Lincoln gave a speech called the **Gettysburg Address.** He gave it to honor the soldiers who had died in the war. He wanted to inspire Americans to keep their country together. He said that a united country and an end to slavery were worth fighting for.

The Tide Turns

The Battle of Gettysburg helped turn the tide of the war in favor of the Union. So did other battles. As part of the Anaconda Plan, the Union wanted to gain control of the Mississippi River. They did this at the **Battle of Vicksburg.** In May 1863 the Union blockaded, or closed off, Vicksburg, Mississippi. Confederate soldiers and citizens faced starvation. The Confederacy surrendered Vicksburg on July 4, 1863, one day after the Battle of Gettysburg ended. The largest number of Civil War battles occurred in Virginia. Many Union soldiers were sent to Virginia. They might have been sent there because the capital of the Confederacy was in Virginia. Also, Washington, D.C., was located between Virginia and Maryland. Union troops might have been sent there to defend the city.

The War Ends

Union General William Tecumseh Sherman helped wear down the Confederate army. He used **total war** to destroy the Confederate soldiers' will to fight. First, Sherman and his troops took Atlanta, Georgia, an important industrial and railway center. Sherman's army marched to take over Savannah, Georgia. They destroyed everything in their path that the South could use to keep fighting. This is called Sherman's "March to the Sea." The Confederacy surrendered in Virginia on April 9, 1865. General Lee and General Grant met in a farmhouse in Appomattox Court House, Virginia, to discuss the terms of surrender. The Civil War was the most destructive war in American history. President Lincoln wanted the country to join together and rebuild itself.

Lesson 3: Review

1. **Main Idea and Details** Fill in the missing details to the main idea.

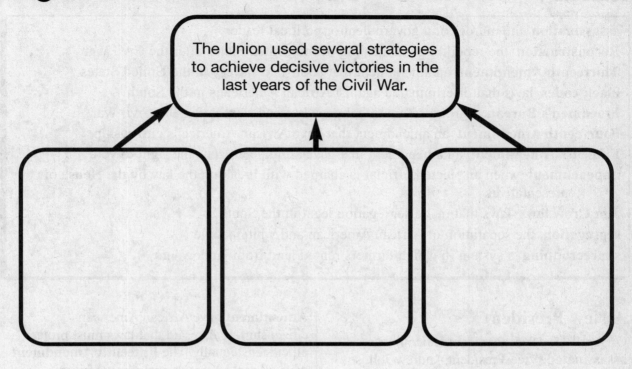

2. What circumstances led the Union to victory on the third day in the Battle of Gettysburg?

_____

_____

3. What were Lincoln's goals as expressed in the Gettysburg Address?

_____

_____

4. **Critical Thinking:** *Interpret Maps* In what state did most of the major battles occur in the Civil War? Give a reason you think this would be so.

_____

_____

_____

5. What was the purpose of total war and Sherman's "March to the Sea"?

_____

_____

Use with pages 516–521.

Lesson 4: The End of Slavery

Vocabulary

assassination the murder of a government or political leader

Reconstruction the rebuilding and healing of the United States after the Civil War

Thirteenth Amendment an amendment that abolished slavery in the United States

black codes laws that discriminated against African Americans in the South

Freedmen's Bureau a group set up to help newly freed slaves after the Civil War

Fourteenth Amendment an amendment that gave African Americans citizenship

Fifteenth Amendment an amendment that gave all male citizens the right to vote

impeachment when an elected official is charged with breaking the law by the House of Representatives

Jim Crow laws laws that made segregation legal in the South

segregation the separation of African American and white people

sharecropping a system in which farmers rented land from landowners

A New President

On April 15, 1865, President Lincoln was **assassinated.** Vice-President Andrew Johnson became President. He wanted to carry out Lincoln's plan for **Reconstruction.** The **Thirteenth Amendment** abolished slavery across the nation on December 18, 1865. Confederate states were to become part of the Union again. Under Johnson's Reconstruction plan, Southern states could pass **black codes.** Black codes took away many rights from African American men. Republican members of Congress did not trust Johnson's Reconstruction plan. They thought it was too easy on the South.

Reconstruction Under Congress

In 1867 Congress passed the first Reconstruction Act. This law made Southern states give African American men the right to vote. People who were Confederate officers or leaders could not vote or hold office. Congress also set up the **Freedmen's Bureau.** Many white Southerners were angry about the laws.

New Amendments

To be readmitted to the Union, Southern states had to accept two amendments. The **Fourteenth** **Amendment** gave African Americans citizenship. It also said that laws must protect all citizens equally. The **Fifteenth Amendment** gave all male citizens, including African American males, the right to vote. President Johnson fought the Fourteenth Amendment and Reconstruction laws. Congress wanted to remove him from office by **impeachment.**

Reconstruction Ends

By 1870 all former Confederate states were readmitted to the Union. New state laws were passed that took away the rights of African Americans. Some states required African Americans to pay a poll tax in order to vote. Some places made African Americans pass a reading test before they could vote. **Jim Crow laws** also **segregated,** or separated, African Americans and whites in public places. Many farmers started **sharecropping.** Many people fell into debt under this system.

After Reconstruction

After Reconstruction, African Americans lost their political power. It would be a long time before African Americans gained the freedoms promised to them during Reconstruction.

Lesson 4: Review

1. 🔄 **Main Idea and Details** Fill in the details to the main idea.

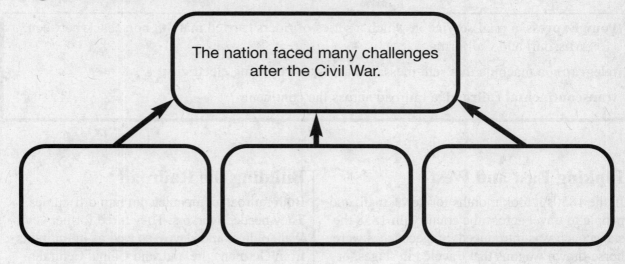

The nation faced many challenges after the Civil War.

2. Why did Republicans in Congress dislike Johnson's Reconstruction plan?

_____

_____

_____

3. **Critical Thinking:** *Cause and Effect* How did the Reconstruction Acts affect the South?

_____

_____

_____

4. Why were three amendments added to the Constitution during Reconstruction?

_____

_____

_____

5. How were the lives of African Americans made more difficult after the end of Reconstruction? Use the word segregation in your answer.

_____

_____

_____

Lesson 1: Rails Across the Nation

Vocabulary

Pony Express a mail service in which a series of riders carried mail on horseback between Missouri and California

telegraph a machine that sent messages across wires using electricity

transcontinental railroad a railroad across the continent

Linking East and West

In the 1850s it took months for news, mail, and people to travel across the country. In 1858 the stagecoach was introduced. Stagecoaches were horse-drawn wagons that traveled in stages, or short sections. They made travel faster. In 1860 the **Pony Express** carried mail from Missouri to California in 10 days. Each express rider rode about 75 miles. Then he handed his mail bags to another rider. The **telegraph** put the Pony Express out of business. This invention could send messages along wires using electricity. The telegraph sent messages across the country in minutes. In October 1861 the first telegraph line across the country was finished. In 1862 the Union Pacific and the Central Pacific companies began building a **transcontinental railroad,** or a railroad across the continent.

Building the Railroad

Both railroad companies ran into difficulties. They needed workers. They hired former Civil War soldiers and slaves, as well as immigrants from Germany, Ireland, and China. Central Pacific workers had a difficult time building tracks over the Sierra Nevada mountain range. Chinese workers did much of the dangerous work. They blasted tunnels through the mountains. Native Americans did not want Union Pacific workers building tracks on their hunting grounds. A Lakota chief named Red Cloud told the railroad workers, "We do not want you here. You are scaring away the buffalo." Soldiers guarded the Union Pacific workers.

The Golden Spike

On May 10, 1869, the tracks of the two railroads met at Promontory Point, Utah Territory. A golden spike was hammered into the track to show the success of the project. People could now travel from coast to coast in less than 10 days. Several other railroad lines soon crossed the West. The railroads brought change and conflict to the United States.

Lesson 1: Review

1. **Sequence** Fill in the missing dates from this diagram.

Pony Express begins delivering mail across the West **1860**

↓

First telegraph line stretches across the United States [ ]

↓

Work on transcontinental railroad begins [ ]

↓

Union Pacific and Central Pacific railroads meet in Utah [ ]

2. What caused the Pony Express to go out of business?

_____

3. Describe the different kinds of problems faced by the Union Pacific and Central Pacific railroads.

_____

_____

4. According to his quote on textbook page 540, why did Red Cloud oppose railroad construction across the Great Plains?

_____

_____

5. **Critical Thinking: *Predict*** What kinds of changes do you think the transcontinental railroad brought to the United States?

_____

_____

Lesson 2: Farmers and Cowboys

Vocabulary

Homestead Act an act that gave free land to pioneers willing to start farms in the Great Plains

homesteaders settlers who claimed land through the Homestead Act

sodbusters farmers in the Great Plains who dug through thick roots to plant crops

exodusters African Americans who left the eastern United States for Kansas and Nebraska

cattle drives when cowboys drove, or moved, huge herds of cattle to railroad lines

barbed wire a twisted wire with sharp points

The Homestead Act

Congress wanted pioneers to move to the Great Plains. In 1862 Congress passed the **Homestead Act.** The Homestead Act gave settlers free land. Settlers had to pay a $10 registration fee. They also had to live on and farm the land for five years. These settlers were called **homesteaders.** The land was hard to farm. Farmers known as **sodbusters** had to dig through several inches of thick, tangled roots to plant crops. They used the soil with the roots, called sod, to build houses.

Life on the Plains

Homesteaders had a hard time growing crops. Winters were cold and summers were hot. Different seasons brought tornadoes, hailstorms, flooding, droughts, prairie fires, blizzards, and ice storms. In the mid-1870s, millions of grasshoppers ate crops in the Great Plains. In 1888 a blizzard called the "schoolchildren's storm" hit Dakota Territory while children were walking home from school.

"America Fever"

More new settlers came to claim land. Hundreds of thousands of people from Europe wanted to come to the Great Plains. They were said to have "America fever." African American homesteaders, called

exodusters, moved to Kansas and Nebraska in search of freer lives. Some exodusters founded the town of Nicodemus, Kansas, in 1877.

The Rise of Cattle Drives

In the mid-1800s, the cattle ranching industry was growing in Texas. Cattle could be sold for high prices in the East. Cowboys went on **cattle drives** to bring the cattle to railroad lines that shipped the cattle east. Abilene, Kansas, was a cowtown, or a town where trains picked cattle up and moved them farther East. In 1871 about 700,000 cows came through Abilene.

Cowboy Life

In 1866 Charles Goodnight and Oliver Loving drove their herd of 2,000 cattle from Texas to Colorado. Their route became known as the Goodnight-Loving Trail. Cowboys worked long and hard. Cattle drives ended by the late 1880s. Farmers fenced off their land with **barbed wire** to keep cattle away. New railroad lines in Texas were used to transport cattle.

Growth in the West

New railroads helped Los Angeles and Seattle grow into important cities by the late 1800s. New settlers, including thousands of Japanese immigrants, built farms in the West.

© Scott Foresman 5

Lesson 2: Review

1. Sequence Put the events in their correct order. Include the year of each event.
   - Homestead Act passed
   - 700,000 longhorns are driven to Abilene, Kansas
   - Dakota Territory hit by "schoolchildren's storm"
   - Goodnight-Loving Trail established
   - Nicodemus, Kansas, founded

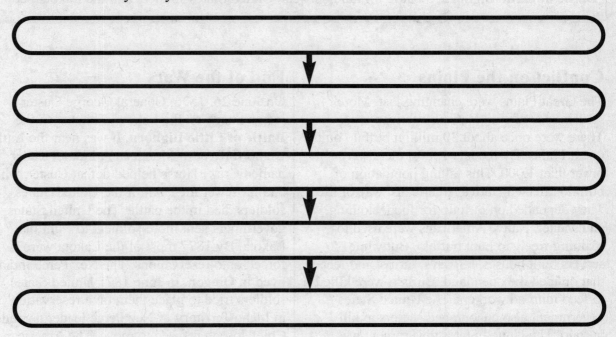

2. What did people have to do to get land through the Homestead Act?

_____

_____

3. Describe three hardships faced by farmers on the Great Plains.

_____

_____

4. **Critical Thinking:** *Decision Making* You know about the difficulties of living and farming on the Great Plains. Would you have wanted to move there? Use the decision-making steps on page H3 in your book.

_____

_____

_____

5. What led to the rise of cattle drives?

_____

_____

Lesson 3: War in the West

Vocabulary

reservation area of land set aside for Native Americans by the United States government

Battle of Little Bighorn a battle for land between United States soldiers and the Lakota people

Conflict on the Plains

The Great Plains were changing fast. More settlers moved onto Native American land. There were once about 30 million buffalo on the Great Plains. By the late 1880s, there were fewer than 1,000. This falling population of buffalo affected Native Americans' way of life. They depended on buffalo for food, clothing, and shelter. Native Americans were used to roaming freely to hunt buffalo. But white settlers built houses, railways, farms, and fences that divided the open land. Buffalo were killed to feed railroad workers. The United States government also encouraged settlers to kill buffalo. The United States government was trying to wipe out a major Native American resource. Government leaders wanted Native Americans to move to **reservations.** In 1868 the United States and the Lakota people signed a treaty that set up the Great Lakota Reservation. The reservation included the Black Hills. In 1874 gold was found in the Black Hills. The United States government offered to buy the land back from the Lakota. The Lakota did not want to sell the land.

End of the Wars

On June 26, 1876, General George Custer led an attack on the Lakota. This began the **Battle of Little Bighorn.** It was near the Little Bighorn River in Montana. A Lakota leader named Crazy Horse helped defeat Custer, who had far fewer men. All of the United States soldiers died in the battle. The United States government sent more soldiers to fight the Lakota. By 1877 most of the Lakota were forced onto reservations. The Nez Percé Indians lived in Oregon. In June 1877 United States soldiers tried to place them on a reservation in Idaho Territory. A Nez Percé leader named Chief Joseph refused to move. The American army fought the Nez Percé for three months. Chief Joseph finally surrendered. By the end of the 1800s, most Native Americans had been forced onto reservations. Today about half of the country's 2.5 million Native Americans live on or near reservations. Many young Native Americans learn the languages of their ancestors. Some tell stories about their people's history in writing and in films.

Lesson 3: Review

1. 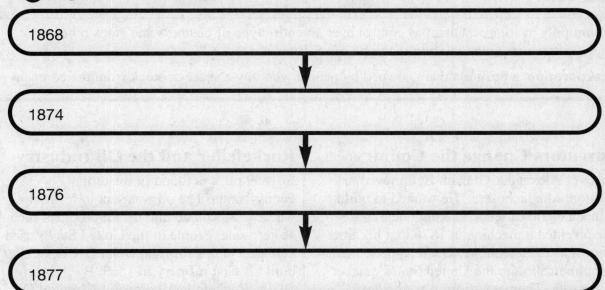 **Sequence** Fill in one key event for each year shown.

| 1868 |
| 1874 |
| 1876 |
| 1877 |

2. How did railroads, farmers, and ranchers affect buffalo on the Great Plains?

_____

_____

3. How did the falling buffalo population affect the Plains Indians?

_____

_____

4. **Critical Thinking:** *Make Inferences* How do you think many Native Americans felt about living on reservations? What evidence can you find in the lesson to support this inference?

_____

_____

5. What are some ways in which Native Americans are keeping their traditions alive today?

_____

_____

Lesson 1: Inventions and Big Business

Vocabulary

monopoly a company that has control over an entire type of business and stops other companies from entering that type of business

corporation a business that is owned by people who buy a share or stock from the company

Inventors Change the Country

In 1871 Alexander Graham Bell moved to Boston, Massachusetts. He wanted to build a machine he called a "talking telegraph." He invented a machine in 1876 that became known as the telephone. The telephone made communication in the United States quicker and easier. Thomas Edison was another inventor. He invented the phonograph, the movie camera, and a light bulb that could burn for two days. In 1879 Lewis Latimer invented a light bulb that lasted much longer. Edison and Latimer made electric light useful for everyone. In 1873 Christopher Latham Sholes invented the first typewriter.

The Rise of Steel

At the beginning of the Industrial Revolution, steel was very expensive to make. In 1856 Henry Bessemer developed a cheaper way to make large amounts of steel. It was called the Bessemer process. Andrew Carnegie began using this process in the 1870s to make steel in Pittsburgh, Pennsylvania. He bought iron mines and used the iron to make steel. He bought railroads to ship resources and his finished products. By 1900 Carnegie made the United States the greatest producer of steel in the world. Carnegie became one of the world's richest people.

Rockefeller and the Oil Industry

In 1859 oil was found in western Pennsylvania. The oil was sent to refineries, where it was made into useful products such as kerosene. People in the United States used kerosene lamps for light. John D. Rockefeller built his first refinery in 1863. By the early 1880s, Rockefeller's company, Standard Oil, had become a **monopoly.** It controlled most of the oil business in the United States. In 1885 the first automobile was invented. By the early 1900s, the automobile created more need for oil products. Refineries started making large amounts of gasoline and motor oil. People began searching the country for oil. Oil was found in Texas, Oklahoma, and California. Other big businesses were also important at this time. This included railroad building and coal mining. Many of these businesses were **corporations.** A corporation is a business that is owned by investors. Investors are people who give money to a company in the hope that they will get more money back later.

A Time of Growth

In the late 1800s, inventions and growing businesses created millions of new jobs. Many people moved to cities to work in industries. Fewer people worked on farms. Immigrants from around the world came to the United States to find jobs.

© Scott Foresman 5

Lesson 1: Review

1. ⟳ **Sequence** Put the events in their correct order. Include the year of each event.
   - John D. Rockefeller builds his first oil refinery
   - Christopher Latham Sholes builds the first typewriter
   - Henry Bessemer develops the Bessemer process
   - The first automobile is built
   - Alexander Graham Bell moves to Boston

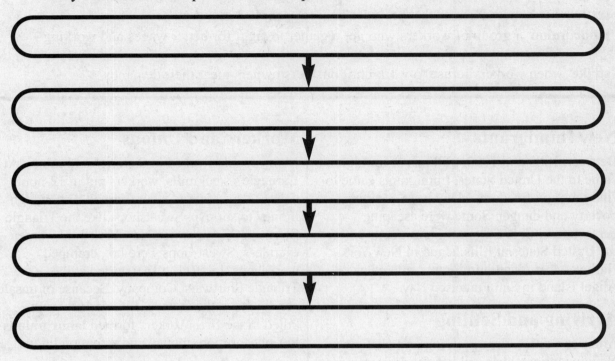

2. How did Alexander Graham Bell's invention affect communication in the United States?

   _____

3. What important invention was made by Henry Bessemer? Why was this invention important?

   _____

4. **Critical Thinking:** *Draw Conclusions* Why do you think Andrew Carnegie bought iron mines and coal mines?

   _____

   _____

5. Why was Rockefeller's Standard Oil Company considered a monopoly?

   _____

   _____

© Scott Foresman 5

Lesson 2: New Americans

Vocabulary

tenement a building that is divided into smaller apartments

prejudice an unfair negative opinion about a group of people

settlement house a center that provides help for people without money

labor union a group of workers who get together to fight for better wages and working conditions

strike when workers refuse to work until business owners meet their demands

New Immigrants

Between 1880 and 1920, millions of immigrants came to the United States. Immigrants came to find jobs and freedom. Many were escaping poverty and hunger. Some were escaping persecution. Most European immigrants entered the United States at Ellis Island in New York Harbor. Most Asian immigrants entered at Angel Island in San Francisco Bay.

Arriving and Settling

American cities were growing and changing. New inventions changed life for many people, including immigrants. In the early 1900s, there were new skyscrapers, subways, and automobiles. Immigrants had to start with almost nothing and find a place to stay and work.

Life in the Cities

Most immigrants moved to cities. There was a shortage of housing. New immigrants crowded into **tenements.** Living was difficult because the apartments in the buildings were very small and many had no heat. Immigrants often faced **prejudice** when looking for work. Many Americans worked to help immigrants improve their lives. Jane Addams started a **settlement house** called Hull House. At the center, immigrants could take English classes and get help finding work.

Workers and Unions

Many people worked in factories and mines. At Carnegie's steel mills, workers put in 12-hour days, 7 days a week. Many earned just enough money to survive. Sweatshops like the Triangle Shirtwaist Company in New York paid women even less. Sweatshops were hot, cramped workshops. In 1911, a fire started at the Triangle Shirtwaist Company. Because of unsafe conditions in the factory, 146 workers were killed in the fire. Workers formed **labor unions** to fight for more money and safer conditions.

Going on Strike

Samuel Gompers fought for workers' rights. He got unions to join together to form the American Federation of Labor, or AFL. The AFL fought for better wages, an eight-hour work day, a safer workplace, and an end to child labor. Unions helped workers **strike** to get what they wanted. Some strikes ended in fights and deaths. Mary Harris Jones, or "Mother Jones," helped miners form unions.

Improving Conditions

Business owners, religious groups, and political leaders also helped make working life better. Working hours were shortened. Workplaces were made safer. Immigrants continued to come to the United States in search of work. A new holiday was created to honor American workers and the work they do. It was called Labor Day. Congress made it a national holiday in 1894.

Lesson 2: Review

1. **Main Idea and Details** Complete the chart below by filling in three details that tell how the United States changed in the late 1800s and early 1900s.

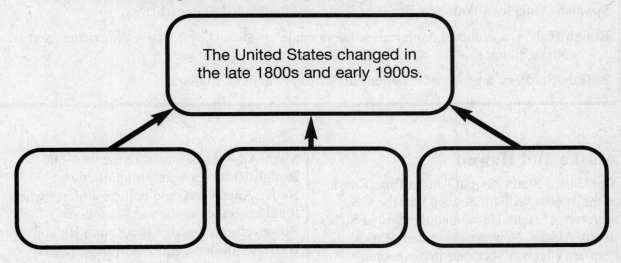

The United States changed in the late 1800s and early 1900s.

2. What are three different reasons that immigrants came to the United States?

_____

_____

_____

3. How did the shortage of housing affect immigrants in American cities?

_____

_____

_____

4. **Critical Thinking:** *Evaluate* Why do you think the Triangle Shirtwaist Company fire might have encouraged people to join labor unions?

_____

_____

_____

5. What is the purpose of Labor Day?

_____

_____

_____

Lesson 3: Expansion Overseas

Vocabulary

Spanish-American War war between Spain and the United States in 1898

Rough Riders a group of American soldiers made up of cowboys, Native Americans, and college athletes

Buffalo Soldiers a group of experienced African American soldiers

Alaska and Hawaii

The United States bought Alaska from Russia in the 1860s. William Seward was the U.S. secretary of state. He wanted the United States to buy Alaska. Newspapers called Alaska "Seward's Icebox" because many people thought it was a frozen wasteland. People changed their minds when gold was discovered there. Many rushed to Alaska in search of gold. During the 1800s American planters began to move to Hawaii. They set up several large plantations by the late 1800s. Queen Liliuokalani ruled Hawaii at this time. She felt that the planters were growing too powerful. American planters led a revolt against the queen. United States soldiers helped the planters. Queen Liliuokalani realized that she could not win. The queen gave up her power. The United States annexed Hawaii in 1898.

The Spanish-American War

In 1895 the people of Cuba revolted against Spanish rule. The Spanish army then put hundreds of thousands of Cubans in prison. The United States felt that Spain was treating the Cuban people unfairly. It also was worried about American businesses in Cuba. The U.S. government sent the battleship USS *Maine* to Cuba. The ship's goal was to protect Americans and their property in Cuba. While in Cuba the *Maine* exploded. Several U.S. newspapers reported that Spain caused the explosion. Congress declared war on Spain in 1898. This began the **Spanish-American War.**

Many Americans fought in the war. The **Rough Riders** were a group of cowboys, Native Americans, and college athletes who fought together in the war. Theodore Roosevelt put together the Rough Riders. **Buffalo Soldiers,** a group of experienced African American soldiers, also fought. The Americans defeated the Spanish quickly. The Spanish were forced to give up many of their colonies around the world. The United States gained control over Puerto Rico, the Philippines, and Guam. The Philippines became an independent nation in 1946.

A New World Power

The United States won the Spanish-American War quickly. This showed other countries that the United States was a world power, or very powerful country. Theodore Roosevelt became a hero. Later he became President of the United States.

Name _____ Date _____ | Lesson 3 Review ⟩

Use with pages 578–582.

Lesson 3: Review

1. **Cause and Effect** Complete this chart by filling in one effect of each event listed below.

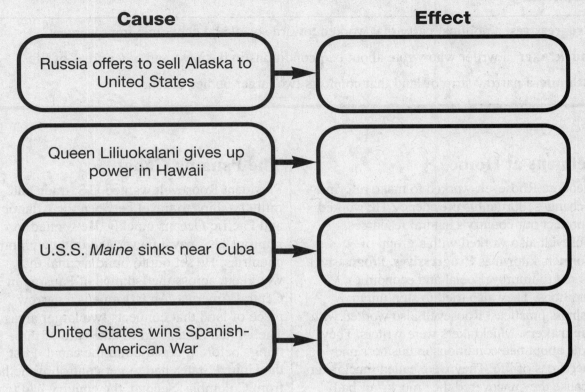

Cause   **Effect**

- Russia offers to sell Alaska to United States →
- Queen Liliuokalani gives up power in Hawaii →
- U.S.S. *Maine* sinks near Cuba →
- United States wins Spanish-American War →

2. Why did newspapers call Alaska "Seward's Icebox"?

_____

_____

3. How did the U.S. military help Hawaii become part of the United States?

_____

_____

4. Who were the Buffalo Soldiers?

_____

_____

5. **Critical Thinking:** *Draw Conclusions* By 1900, the United States was seen as a world power. How do you think the events described in the lesson helped the United States become a world power?

_____

_____

© Scott Foresman 5

Quick Study   Unit 8, Chapter 17, Lesson 3 Review **123**

Lesson 1: A Time of Reforms

Vocabulary

Progressives a political party that worked toward social and economic improvement

muckraker a writer who wrote about bad conditions in business and other areas of life

isthmus a narrow strip of land that connects two larger bodies of land

Reforms at Home

Theodore Roosevelt worked to make reforms, or changes, during his presidency. He worked to protect our country's natural resources. Roosevelt also worked with a group of reformers known as **Progressives.** Progressives worked to improve social and economic conditions. They also tried to stop unfair business practices. Roosevelt also worked with **muckrakers.** Muckrakers were writers. They wrote about bad conditions in business and other areas of life. They were called muckrakers because they uncovered the "muck," or bad conditions, in society. Ida Tarbell and Upton Sinclair were muckrakers. Ida Tarbell wrote about companies that joined together to control an industry. These large companies were called "trusts." Upton Sinclair wrote about meat-packing plants that were dirty and dangerous to work in. This caused Roosevelt to sign two reform acts—The Meat Inspection Act and the Pure Food and Drug Act. Roosevelt also became a "trust-buster." He used the Sherman Antitrust Act of 1890 to force trusts to break into smaller companies. These acts allowed the government to inspect companies and stop unfair business practices.

The Panama Canal

President Roosevelt wanted U.S. trade and military ships to travel between the Atlantic and Pacific Oceans quickly. He wanted to improve U.S. naval power and trade with other countries. He set out to build a canal that would cut across the Isthmus of Panama in Central America. An **isthmus** is a narrow piece of land that connects two larger areas. The United States had to take care of three things before it could build the canal. First, the United States had to get control of the land from Colombia. Second, the country had to find a way to control mosquitoes in the area. These insects carried diseases such as malaria and yellow fever. Third, the United States had to find a way to dig through the muddy, swampy, and mountainous land. Roosevelt found solutions to all these problems. The Panama Canal was completed in 1914.

© Scott Foresman 5

Lesson 1: Review

1. ⟳ **Summarize** Complete the chart to summarize the major events of the presidency of Theodore Roosevelt.

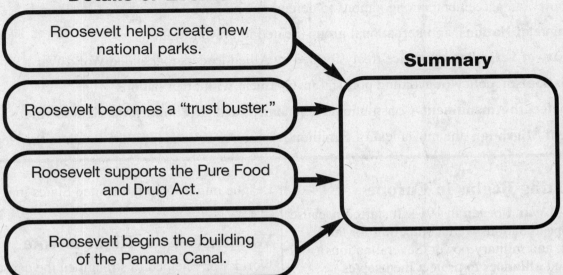

Details or Events

Roosevelt helps create new national parks.

Roosevelt becomes a "trust buster."

Roosevelt supports the Pure Food and Drug Act.

Roosevelt begins the building of the Panama Canal.

Summary

2. **Critical Thinking:** *Evaluate* Do you think "muckraker" is a good term to describe writers like Ida Tarbell and Upton Sinclair? Explain.

_____

_____

3. Describe three reforms supported by Theodore Roosevelt.

_____

_____

4. Why did the United States want to build a canal across Panama?

_____

_____

5. Describe the problems the United States faced in building the Panama Canal.

_____

_____

Lesson 2: World War I

Vocabulary

World War I a war between many countries around the world; 1914–1918

alliance an agreement among nations to defend one another

League of Nations an international group created to prevent wars

Treaty of Versailles the peace treaty formed by Allied leaders that ended World War I

isolationism policy of avoiding political involvement with other nations

Nineteenth Amendment Constitutional amendment that gave women the right to vote

Great Migration the movement of 5 million African Americans from the South to the North

Fighting Begins in Europe

World War I began in 1914. It started because European nations were competing for land, trade, and military power. Several nations formed **alliances** to protect themselves from enemy attacks. There were two major alliances. The Allied Powers included Britain, France, and Russia. The Central Powers were led by Germany, Austria-Hungary, and Turkey.

The United States Enters the War

Certain events in 1917 caused the United States to join with the Allied Powers. First, the United States learned of a telegram that Germany sent to Mexico, asking Mexico to join the Central Powers. In return, Germany promised to help Mexico get back lands it had lost to the United States. Then, German submarines attacked and sank three American trade ships.

The War Ends

The fresh American troops helped the Allied Powers defeat the Central Powers in 1918. In January 1919 President Wilson and Allied leaders met in Versailles, France, to write a peace treaty. Wilson wanted a treaty that did not punish the Central Powers and included a **League of Nations.** The **Treaty of Versailles** set up the League but punished the Central Powers. The U.S. Senate did not approve the treaty because many Americans feared that the

League might force the United States into future wars. They wanted **isolationism.**

Women Get the Right to Vote

World War I helped to strengthen the cause for women's suffrage. As men joined the armed forces, women replaced them in the workforce. Women argued that they had earned the right to vote. In 1919 Congress passed the **Nineteenth Amendment** to the Constitution. By August 1920, the states approved the amendment and it became law.

The Great Migration

Between 1915 and the 1940s, millions of African Americans moved from the South to the North. This was called the **Great Migration.** Because of World War I, the demand for workers in factories grew. Many African Americans left their farms and headed north. However, when they moved to the North they still faced segregation and discrimination.

Fighting Discrimination

Ida Wells-Barnett was an African American leader in Chicago. She started one of the first suffrage groups for African American women. She helped start an African American newspaper. She also won the battle against segregation on buses and trains in Illinois.

© Scott Foresman 5

Lesson 2 Review

1. **Summarize** Complete the chart to summarize the changes brought about by World War I.

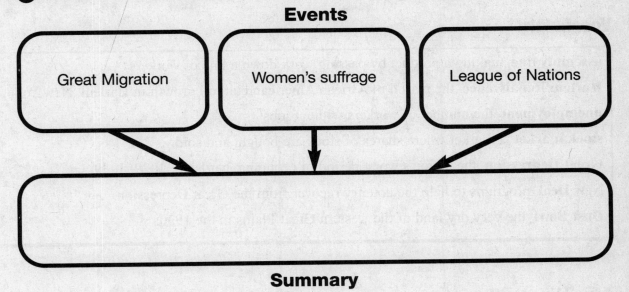

Events

| Great Migration | Women's suffrage | League of Nations |

Summary

2. Identify the two alliances that fought each other in World War I.

_____

_____

3. What role did the United States play in World War I?

_____

_____

4. **Critical Thinking:** *Problem Solving* Identify a problem in the news today and suggest a possible solution. Use the problem-solving steps on page H3 in your textbook.

_____

_____

5. What was the effect of the Great Migration on African Americans in the United States?

_____

_____

Lesson 3: Times of Plenty, Times of Hardship

Vocabulary

assembly line making a product by passing work down a line of workers

Harlem Renaissance the period of African American cultural growth in Harlem, New York

unemployment the number of workers without jobs

stock market a market where shares of stock are bought and sold

Great Depression the nation's worst period of economic hardship; 1929–1939

New Deal programs to help the country recover from the Great Depression

Dust Bowl the very dry land of the western Great Plains in the 1930s

New Ways to Travel

In 1903 Wilbur and Orville Wright made the first successful powered airplane flight. The airplane industry grew. Henry Ford found a way to make cars that many people could afford. He used an **assembly line.** Workers then could make cars more quickly and for less money. This allowed many Americans to buy cars and move around more freely.

The Roaring Twenties

The 1920s was a period of strong economic growth. People called this period the "Roaring Twenties." New forms of entertainment were invented. African Americans in Harlem, New York, also experienced a time of economic and cultural growth. This was called the **Harlem Renaissance.**

The Great Crash

Unemployment grew after World War I. Many Americans tried to make money in the **stock market.** In 1929 the stock market crashed. This means stock prices fell quickly. Many people lost their money. The United States entered a period known as the **Great Depression.**

The New Deal

Franklin D. Roosevelt became President in 1933. He worked with Congress to develop the **New Deal.** Many New Deal programs found work for people who lost their jobs. One program was the Civilian Conservation Corps, or CCC. Men worked to conserve forests and other natural resources. Some other programs helped the banking system. The Social Security Act was passed to give money to the unemployed and the elderly.

The Dust Bowl

In the Great Plains, very dry weather caused the **Dust Bowl.** Rich farmland turned to dust. Many farmers left their useless land to travel west to California. They hoped to find work and better lives.

Hard Times Continue

The Great Depression continued. Few people who were unemployed in 1932 had found jobs by 1935. However, the New Deal helped many people to survive until the economy improved. Because of Roosevelt's reforms, the government became more powerful.

Lesson 3 Review

1. **Summarize** Write the details for the following summary.

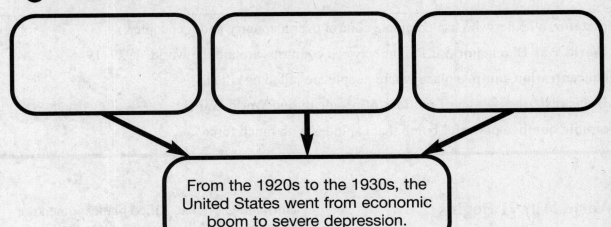

From the 1920s to the 1930s, the United States went from economic boom to severe depression.

2. What system of making products did Henry Ford develop, and how did it affect the nation?

_____

_____

_____

3. **Critical Thinking:** *Compare and Contrast* Compare American life in the "Roaring Twenties" with American life in the Great Depression of the 1930s.

_____

_____

_____

4. Describe two New Deal programs.

_____

_____

_____

5. Why did Dust Bowl farmers move to California?

_____

_____

_____

Lesson 4: World War II

Use with pages 624–630.

Vocabulary

dictator a leader who has complete control over a country and its people

World War II a major war fought between countries around the world; 1939–1945

concentration camp a place where people are jailed or killed

Holocaust the murder of millions of people during World War II

atomic bomb a powerful bomb that explodes with much force

World War II Begins

Economic hardship hit Europe as well. This helped leaders called **dictators** gain control over some countries. Germany, Italy, and Japan formed an alliance. They wanted to take over other countries around the world. Their alliance became known as the Axis. In Western Europe, Britain and France were against the Axis. They formed an alliance called the Allies. Germany attacked Poland in 1939. Then Britain and France declared war on Germany. This began **World War II.**

Americans at War

The Soviet Union joined the Allies in 1941. On December 7, 1941, Japanese planes bombed American navy ships at Pearl Harbor, Hawaii. The United States declared war on Japan. Germany and Italy declared war on the United States. The United States joined the Allies. As men joined the military, women replaced them in the factories. The U.S. government became afraid that enemies were living in the United States. Because of the government's fears, many German, Italian, and Japanese people living in the United States were arrested. The U.S. government forced many Japanese Americans to live in relocation camps.

Victory in Europe

On June 6, 1944, thousands of Allied soldiers from Britain invaded the beaches of Normandy, France. Allied planes joined the invasion. The Allied forces drove the Germans east, out of Western Europe. Soviet troops also pushed the Germans west. The Germans finally surrendered on May 8, 1945. Allied troops began to free Europe. They found that Nazis had built **concentration camps** all over Europe. Nazis imprisoned Jews and other people in these camps. About 12 million people were killed in the concentration camps. This widespread murder is called the **Holocaust.**

Victory in Asia

The U.S. government worried that an invasion into Japan could cost many American lives. President Truman learned about a powerful, new weapon—the **atomic bomb.** It was thousands of times more powerful than an ordinary bomb. On August 6, 1945, the United States dropped an atomic bomb onto Hiroshima, Japan. A few days later, the United States dropped a second bomb on the city of Nagasaki, killing thousands more Japanese. Japan surrendered on August 14, 1945, ending World War II.

The Costs of War

World War II was the bloodiest war in history. Most of the world's nations took part in this war. Countries around the world now had something new to worry about—the deadly atomic bomb.

Lesson 4 Review

1. **Summarize** Write a sentence that summarizes the details below.

Events

| Thousands of Americans died in the Japanese attack on Pearl Harbor. | Millions were imprisoned and killed in Nazi concentration camps during World War II. | Nearly 80,000 Japanese died when the U.S. dropped an atomic bomb on Hiroshima. |

Summary

2. What major nations fought in World War II and why?

_____

_____

3. How did the United States government react to the bombing of Pearl Harbor?

_____

_____

4. What strategies did the Allies use in Europe and the Pacific?

_____

_____

5. **Critical Thinking:** *Make Generalizations* Describe some of the terrible effects of World War II on civilians.

_____

_____

Lesson 1: A Dangerous World

Vocabulary

United Nations an organization of nations that works toward peace

communism a political and economic system in which the government owns all businesses and land

Cold War the struggle between the United States and the Soviet Union and their different ways of life

Iron Curtain the line that divided Europe into communist and noncommunist countries

Korean War the war between communist North Korea and noncommunist South Korea

Cuban Missile Crisis the discovery that the Soviet Union had nuclear missiles in Cuba

arms race a race between nations to build powerful weapons

A New Kind of War

In 1945, 50 nations met to form the **United Nations.** Its goal was to find peaceful solutions to international problems. The two most powerful nations, the United States and the Soviet Union, joined the United Nations. The Soviet Union had **communism**. The United States believed in a democratic government and free enterprise. American leaders wanted to stop the spread of communism. The two nations entered into the **Cold War.**

The Iron Curtain Falls

The Soviet Union controlled Eastern Europe. Under Soviet rule each nation was ordered to set up a communist government that was loyal to the Soviet Union. The dividing line separating communist and noncommunist countries in Europe was called the **Iron Curtain.** President Truman worked to strengthen the noncommunist nations of Western Europe.

Cold War Conflicts

After World War II ended, Korea was divided into North Korea and South Korea. With the Soviet Union's help, North Korea set up a communist government. On June 25, 1950, North Korean forces invaded South Korea. President Truman wanted to help stop the spread of communism. He sent American troops into South Korea. The **Korean War** had begun.

The Cuban Missile Crisis

In 1959 Cuba became the first communist country in the Western Hemisphere. In 1962 the United States discovered that the Soviets were setting up nuclear missiles in Cuba. This became known as the **Cuban Missile Crisis.** President John F. Kennedy told the American people about the crisis. Then he demanded that the Soviet Union remove their missiles. He said that the U.S. Navy would block Soviet ships from bringing more nuclear weapons into Cuba.

The Arms Race Continues

The United States and the Soviet Union continued their **arms race.** They raced to build stronger and more dangerous weapons. U.S. leaders thought it was important to stay ahead of the Soviets. They believed that if the United States had stronger weapons than the Soviets, the Soviets would not attack.

© Scott Foresman 5

Lesson 1: Review

1. 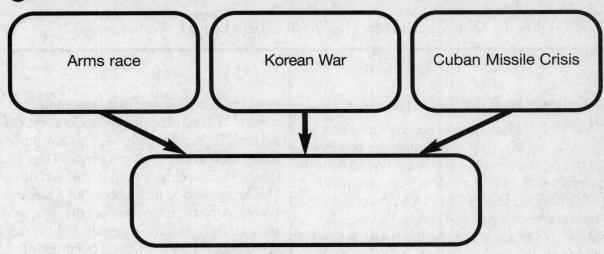 **Summarize** Complete the chart below by summarizing three key Cold War events.

2. What differences between the United States and the Soviet Union led to the beginning of the Cold War?

_____

_____

_____

3. Why did Truman believe the United States should fight in the Korean War?

_____

_____

_____

4. What actions did Kennedy take after Soviet missiles were discovered in Cuba?

_____

_____

_____

5. **Critical Thinking:** *Express Ideas* Do you believe it was important for the United States to stay ahead of the Soviet Union in the arms race? Explain.

_____

_____

_____

Lesson 2: Struggle for Equal Rights

Vocabulary

civil rights the basic rights that are given to all citizens by the Constitution

Struggle to End Segregation

In 1948 President Truman ended segregation in the U.S. military. But segregation still continued in public places, especially in the South. African American and white children were separated into different schools. The NAACP worked to end school segregation. Thurgood Marshall was a civil rights lawyer for the NAACP. **Civil rights** are the basic rights that are given to all citizens by the Constitution. Marshall took on the case of an African American student named Linda Brown. She was not allowed to attend the school a few blocks from her home. Instead, Brown had to take the bus to an African American school. In 1954 the Supreme Court ruled that segregation in public schools was illegal under the Constitution.

The Montgomery Bus Boycott

Under Alabama law African Americans had to sit in the back of city buses. Rosa Parks was an African American who challenged that law in 1955. Parks refused to move to the back of a city bus. She was arrested. Parks's arrest angered many African American leaders. Martin Luther King, Jr., was a civil rights leader. He believed in nonviolent and peaceful protest. Jo Ann Robinson and other African American leaders organized a bus boycott. King was a leader in the boycott. Parks's case went to the Supreme Court. In 1956 the Court ruled against segregation on public buses.

Gains and Losses

In August 1963 Martin Luther King, Jr., led tens of thousands of Americans in a peaceful march into Washington, D.C. They wanted Congress to pass President Kennedy's civil rights bill.

President Kennedy was assassinated in November 1963. The next year Congress passed the Civil Rights Act of 1964. This law made segregation in public places illegal. Then Congress passed the Voting Rights Act of 1965. This law protected the rights of all Americans to vote. African Americans had the right to vote before this. But many were kept from voting in the South. This law helped hundreds of thousands of African Americans vote for the first time. Malcolm X was a civil rights leader. He thought that civil rights laws would not bring changes quickly enough. He believed that white Americans would never fully support equal rights for African Americans. He wanted African Americans to rely on themselves. Both Malcolm X and Martin Luther King, Jr., were assassinated in the 1960s.

Equal Rights for Women

The number of women who worked grew during the 1950s. Yet women often earned less than men. Many types of jobs were not open to women. In 1966 the National Organization for Women, or NOW, was formed. It fought for fair pay and equal opportunities for women. In 1968 Shirley Chisholm became the first African American woman in Congress. In 1981 Sandra Day O'Connor became the first woman to serve on the Supreme Court.

Working for a Change

Many different groups worked for social change. Native American leaders worked to improve social and economic conditions for Native Americans. Mexican American leaders such as César Chávez and Dolores Huerta fought for the rights of migrant farm workers.

© Scott Foresman 5

Lesson 2: Review

1. **Cause and Effect** Complete the chart below by filling in the effects of several major events of the Civil Rights Movement.

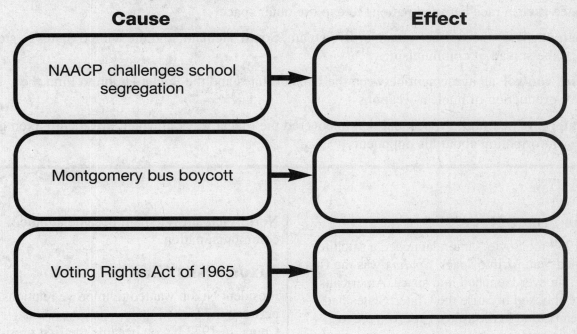

Cause   **Effect**

NAACP challenges school segregation →

Montgomery bus boycott →

Voting Rights Act of 1965 →

2. What civil rights lawyer won the case that outlawed segregation in schools?

_____

_____

3. Describe the roles of Rosa Parks, Jo Ann Robinson, and Martin Luther King, Jr., in the Montgomery bus boycott.

_____

_____

4. **Critical Thinking:** *Compare and Contrast* How did the views of Malcolm X differ from those of Martin Luther King, Jr.?

_____

_____

5. What were some goals of the women's rights movement of the 1960s and 1970s?

_____

_____

Lesson 3: The Cold War Continues

Vocabulary

space race a race between nations to explore outer space

Vietnam War the war between North Vietnam, South Vietnam, and the United States to stop the spread of communism

arms control an agreement between the United States and the Soviet Union to limit the production of nuclear weapons

Watergate Scandal the scandal that uncovered the illegal ways in which President Nixon got information about his opponents

The Space Race

In 1957 the Soviet Union launched a satellite named *Sputnik* into space. *Sputnik* was the first satellite ever launched into space. Americans were shocked because the United States had fallen behind in the **space race,** or race to explore outer space. Americans did not want the Soviet Union to know more about exploring space. In 1961 the Soviet Union sent the first astronaut into space to orbit, or circle, Earth. In 1969 the United States became the first country to send people to the moon.

The Vietnam War

In 1954 Vietnam won its independence from France. But the war divided Vietnam into North Vietnam and South Vietnam. North Vietnam had a communist government. North Vietnam wanted to unite with South Vietnam under one communist government. South Vietnam fought the communists. President Lyndon B. Johnson wanted to stop North Vietnam's communist invasion. In 1964 Johnson sent American soldiers into Vietnam. This was the beginning of the **Vietnam War.** Americans were divided over whether to support the war. People who supported the war were called "hawks." People who were against the war were called "doves." American troops stopped fighting the North Vietnamese in 1973. In 1975 South Vietnam surrendered to

North Vietnam. Vietnam became a united communist nation.

Nixon Visits China

President Nixon wanted to improve relations between the United States and communist China. In 1972 Nixon became the first president to visit China. The trip was a big step toward better relations with China. That same year Nixon traveled to the Soviet Union. He met with Soviet leaders to sign an **arms control** agreement. This agreement limited the number of nuclear weapons each nation could have. It helped improve relations between the two nations. The **Watergate Scandal** ended Nixon's presidency. Five men were caught breaking into a government office. They were looking for information about Nixon's political enemies. Evidence showed that Nixon had done illegal things to hide information about the break-in. On August 9, 1974, Nixon became the only President to resign from office.

Tensions Rise Again

Jimmy Carter became President in 1976. He also hoped to improve relations with communist countries. But in December 1979, the Soviet Union invaded Afghanistan. Carter spoke against the invasion. Because of this invasion, Cold War tensions were on the rise again between the United States and the Soviet Union.

© Scott Foresman 5

Lesson 3: Review

1. ⟳ **Summarize** Complete the chart below by summarizing these key Cold War events.

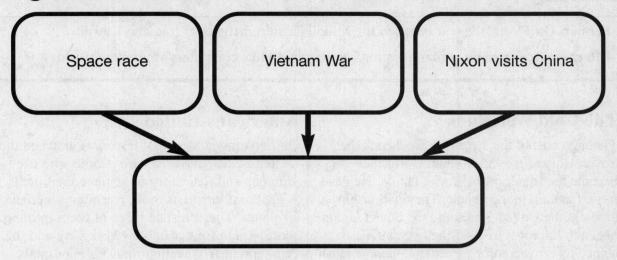

2. How did the success of *Sputnik* affect the space race?

_____

_____

_____

3. **Critical Thinking:** *Point of View* Was President Johnson a hawk or a dove? Explain how you reached your answer.

_____

_____

_____

4. How did President Nixon's trip to China affect relations between the United States and China?

_____

_____

_____

5. Were Cold War tensions rising or falling as the 1980s began? Explain.

_____

_____

_____

Lesson 4: Looking Toward the Future

Vocabulary

Persian Gulf War the war between the Middle Eastern nations of Iraq and Kuwait

Internet an electronic communications system that links computers around the world

The Cold War Ends

The high cost of the arms race weakened the Soviet Union. In 1985 Mikhail Gorbachev became the leader of the Soviet Union. He gave more freedom to the people. The relationship between the United States and the Soviet Union began to improve. In 1987 the two nations signed an arms control agreement. George Bush became President in 1989. He worked with Gorbachev to end the Cold War. Democratic governments began replacing communist governments in Eastern Europe. In 1991 the Soviet Union split apart. The Cold War was over.

A New Role in the World

After the breakup of the Soviet Union, the United States became the world's only superpower. It faced new challenges, such as whether to use its powers to end conflicts around the world. In 1990 Iraq invaded Kuwait. In January 1991 the United States led an alliance of over 20 nations in an attack to drive Iraq out of Kuwait. This was the **Persian Gulf War.**

The End of a Century

The presidential election of 2000 was one of the closest in American history. George W. Bush became President in 2001. The **Internet** started as a result of the Cold War. During the 1960s the United States wanted to build a communication system that would work after a nuclear attack and scientists came up with the idea to link computers together. Today the Internet is used by millions of people around the world.

Americans United

On September 11, 2001, terrorists attacked the United States. Terrorists are people who use violence and fear to try to achieve their goals. A group of terrorists took over four American airplanes. They crashed three of them into the World Trade Center in New York City and the Pentagon near Washington, D.C. Thousands of people were killed. The American people united, and many risked their lives to save others. Leaders from many nations, including the Prime Minister of Great Britain, joined the fight against terrorism.

The Struggle Against Terrorism

In 2001 the United States attacked in Afghanistan and overthrew the government which had refused to capture the terrorists in their country. The United States and its allies attacked Iraq in 2003 because it refused to cooperate fully with United Nations weapons inspectors. As in Afghanistan, the regime lost power, and rebuilding and the establishment of democracy began.

Rebuilding at Home

Plans were made for new buildings and a memorial at the World Trade Center. The Department of Homeland Security was begun.

Looking Ahead

Do you have any predictions about the future? Will we succeed in ending terrorism? What do you think will be the most important invention of the twenty-first century? Will there be new medicines? Will we find new ways to conserve natural resources and protect our environment?

© Scott Foresman 5

Lesson 4: Review

1. **Main Idea and Details** Complete the chart below by listing three major changes that have taken place since the early 1980s.

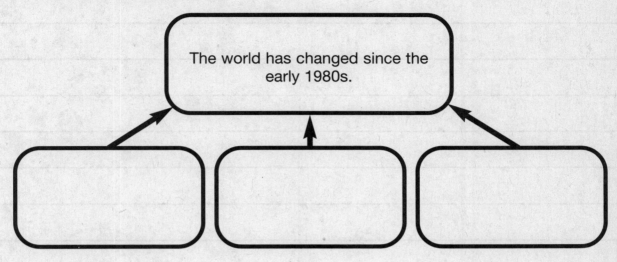

The world has changed since the early 1980s.

2. Did relations between the United States and the Soviet Union improve during the 1980s? Explain.

   _____

   _____

3. How did the Cold War help lead to the development of the Internet?

   _____

   _____

4. Following the terrorist attacks of September 11, 2001, did the United States act alone in battling terrorism? Explain.

   _____

   _____

5. **Critical Thinking:** *Predict* Reread the list of questions on this page. Pick one of these questions, or write a question of your own about the future. Then write a one-page paper, answering the question with your predictions for the future.

   _____

   _____

NOTES

NOTES

NOTES